*Law*Basics

# AN INTRODUCTION TO THE STUDY OF LAW

By

Simon Halliday
*Professor in York Law School at the University of York*

<table>
<tr><td>T.T. Arvind<br>*Professor of Law,*<br>*University of Newcastle*</td><td>John Gardner<br>*Professor of Jurisprudence at*<br>*Oxford University and a Fellow*<br>*of University College*</td></tr>
<tr><td>Donald Nicolson<br>*Professor of Law,*<br>*University of Strathclyde*</td><td>Peter Robson<br>*Professor of Law,*<br>*University of Strathclyde*</td></tr>
<tr><td>Jenny Steele<br>*Professor in York Law School,*<br>*University of York*</td><td>Prue Vines<br>*Professor of Law,*<br>*University of New South Wales*</td></tr>
</table>

**W. GREEN**

**THOMSON REUTERS**

Published in 2012 by W. Green,
21 Alva Street, Edinburgh EH2 4PS
Part of Thomson Reuters (Professional) UK Limited
(Registered in England & Wales, Company No 1679046.
Registered Office and address for service:
2nd Floor, 1 Mark Square, Leonard Street, London EC2A 4EG)

www.wgreen.co.uk

*Typeset by Alex Nashed, W. Green, Edinburgh*
*Printed in Great Britain CPI Group (UK) Ltd, Croydon CR0 4YY*

No natural forests were destroyed to make this product;
Only farmed timber was used and replanted

A CIP catalogue record for this book is available from the British Library

ISBN 978-0-414-01869-3

To the memory of Mark Halliday

# ACKNOWLEDGEMENTS

This book is for students, both undergraduates and post-graduates, who are about to study law for the first time or have just begun to do so. The idea for the book grew out of a course which I developed for law students at Strathclyde University in Glasgow. There was a strong sense that, because legal research has diversified somewhat in recent years and become quite a varied business, students needed some kind of a "map" of legal scholarship at the very outset of their studies to help them navigate their way through their law degrees. The original idea for turning that course into a small book for a wider readership came from my former colleague Dot Reid, now of Glasgow University's Law School. It was a characteristically good idea of Dot's and I am very grateful to her for it. The course which sparked the book idea was delivered by a range of my former colleagues at Strathclyde University and the plan was to convert their introductory lectures into chapters. For various good reasons to do with work pressures, quite a few of the original contributors to the course had to drop out of the book project. I am nonetheless very grateful to them: John Blackie, Sylvie da Lomba, Mary Neale, and Kenneth Norrie.

Janet Campbell of Thomson Reuters has been a very helpful and patient commissioning editor (which is no bad thing given that the manuscript arrived on her desk later than I had faithfully promised it would). Thanks are due to her too.

Given that the inspiration of this book was the teaching team and course based at Strathclyde University Law School, it is appropriate that all the royalties from the sales of this book are to be donated to Strathclyde University's charity, The Malawi Millennium Project.

Simon Halliday
York, June 2012

# ACKNOWLEDGEMENTS

# CONTENTS

# NOTE ON CONTRIBUTORS

**T.T. Arvind** is a Professor of Law at the University of Newcastle.

**Donald Nicolson** is a Professor of Law at the University of Strathclyde.

**John Gardner** is Professor of Jurisprudence at Oxford University and a Fellow of University College.

**Simon Halliday** is a Professor in York Law School at the University of York.

**Peter Robson** is a Professor of Law at the University of Strathclyde.

**Jenny Steele** is a Professor in York Law School at the University of York.

**Prue Vines** is a Professor of Law at the University of New South Wales.

# INTRODUCTION

*Simon Halliday*

This book is designed to help students who have recently started studying law, or are about to do so. It does not tell you how to study law so much as it tells you about the study of law. There are plenty of textbooks which help law students navigate their way around a law library, or give helpful advice on how to read court judgments and statutes. This book, however, does something different, though equally important. It gives you an introduction to the different ways in which law is studied. Studying law is now quite a varied business. Inside law schools you will find lecturers and professors drawing from a wide range of other academic disciplines to study law. Indeed, quite a few law lecturers and professors have been trained in other disciplines and do not have law degrees themselves. The variety of scholarship that you will encounter in studying law is one of the features of legal study which makes it so enjoyable and rewarding. Law degrees, at both undergraduate and postgraduate levels, are no longer just about training people for the legal profession. Many students who graduate with a degree from a law school do not use it for legal practice. Law schools are now places of general and academic learning, not simply of vocational training, and this is reflected in the different approaches to legal study which are found in them. Rather than thinking of law as a specific academic discipline in its own right, it is probably better to see it as a focus of study from a rich variety of disciplinary traditions. Indeed, we might call it a "rendezvous subject",[i] in the sense that law is a site where different kinds of scholar meet to debate and share insights about what law is, what it stipulates, how it operates, and so forth. So the aim of this book is to offer you an accessible introduction to the varieties of legal scholarship which make up the curricula of law degrees at both undergraduate and postgraduate level—to provide you with a "map", if you like, of legal scholarship.

**The approach of this book and how you should read it**
This book provides you with one of the essential building blocks for studying law. An understanding of the "map" of legal scholarship will form part of the foundation of your legal knowledge. So this book is introductory and, as I mentioned earlier, targeted at those who are beginning or about to begin legal study of some kind. Because of this, it has been written in a way which (we hope) you will find very easy to read. Unlike other books which you will encounter in your legal studies, this book is light on references to other scholarly work. This is a deliberate strategy on our part. We do not want you to be distracted by references or citations. Many academic books, as you will soon discover, need to be worked through slowly. Some authors use their books to engage in debates with other authors or various schools of thought. These kinds of books need to be heavy on references and citations and the student reader should keep an

eye on them in order to fully grasp exactly how the author is advancing knowledge within a particular field of scholarship. Other books are written as a kind of compendium of detailed reference points about law and are intended for readers to dip in and out of, as and when needed, without ever having to read the book as a whole. Often, the student reader will have to follow up these reference points in other books, case law or statutes in order to come to his or her own view on a particular legal question.

This book, however, is quite different. We want you to read the whole thing, but to be able to do so fairly quickly and very easily. It is the sort of book to take to the coffee house or pub rather than to pore over in a library. Although this might be stretching the point (or might be overly pessimistic) this book could be one of the few opportunities (perhaps even the only one) to read for pleasure at a leisurely pace as part of your legal studies. Each chapter will have some references to other work at the end which you can follow up should you want to. However, you should finish the whole book before doing so. Get the basic idea of the map of legal scholarship in your head first before following up those references to deepen your knowledge. You will certainly need to deepen your knowledge over time—this book is merely introductory, after all—but you should start that process only once you have grasped the basic ideas in the first place. In other words, use this book as an initial foundation.

**An overview of the "map"**
The task of describing the various approaches to legal study which make up the "map" of legal scholarship is not, unfortunately, absolutely straightforward. There is no clear agreement amongst legal scholars about how to do this. Much has been made, for example, of the difference between what are called "doctrinal" or "black letter" approaches to law on the one hand and, on the other, what is sometimes called a "law in context", "law in action" or "socio-legal" approach. At a very basic level this distinction certainly says something about how legal scholarship has evolved in the United Kingdom over the last 50 years or so. In essence, the distinction points to the fact that contemporary legal scholarship has moved beyond technical legal analysis to embrace a social scientific approach to the study of law. Whereas legal scholarship used to be characterised by the exposition of positive law, isolated from its economic, political and cultural contexts—a kind of dry and technical legal analysis—it is far more common now for legal scholars to examine those economic, political and cultural contexts in which law is created, applied and understood. Indeed, as the chapter on empirical approaches demonstrates, many legal scholars use the research methods of the social sciences to do so. Nonetheless, the distinction between "black letter" approaches and "socio-legal" approaches to legal study is probably too crude to be all that helpful. They are pretty broad categories and, because of that, they risk obscuring more than they reveal. Equally, although this might be a controversial view, there are probably more socio-legal sensibilities amongst so-called black letter lawyers, and more black letter law within socio-legal scholarship than either set of proponents might care to admit.

Our preference, then, is to avoid large-scale binary divisions and instead to draw up a longer list of various approaches to legal study. Although you must read the chapters that follow in order to understand the various approaches to law which characterise modern legal study, it may be useful to give a very brief overview of the typology at this stage. The book begins with a discussion of doctrinal approaches to the study of law. Doctrinal study is probably what most novice students of law imagine law school to involve. It is a long-standing and traditional approach to legal study which concerns the internal coherence of legal concepts and legal reasoning. It involves the sort of legal reasoning that one might expect to see in appeal court proceedings where the debate is about what the correct legal interpretation of a situation is—looking at law from the inside, as it were—applying legal rules and principles to various scenarios. Philosophical approaches to the study of law use philosophical methods of reasoning to consider the nature and validity of law. Classic questions would include "What is law?", "What it is that makes law different from morality or politics?", or "How far are ethics or morality part of legal reasoning?" Equally, legal scholars might use philosophical methods to assess legal principles and concepts against certain standards such as justice, fairness or ethics. Empirical approaches to law, by way of contrast, seek to understand the functioning and operations of law in society. They use the research methods of the social sciences to explore questions such as "How and why were laws created to have particular content?", "How is law implemented and what happens to it in the implementation process?", "How is the legal system used?", and "What effects does law have in society?" Critical approaches to the study of law—what is often called "critical legal theory"—are an interesting kind of blend of philosophical and empirical approaches. In many ways, critical approaches to law use philosophical methods to raise empirical questions about discrimination and oppression through law. They examine the ways in which law—while often appearing to do the opposite—actually works to the disadvantage of certain groups in society such as black and minority ethnic groups, the working class and women. Popular cultural approaches to law draw from the research traditions of the humanities and examine how law is understood and portrayed through cultural media such as literature, film and television. The study of law through popular culture is probably the newest approach within our typology, but is now sufficiently established within UK legal scholarship that it deserves a place in our scheme.

These five approaches—doctrinal, philosophical, empirical, critical and popular cultural—represent the main landmarks on our map of legal scholarship. However, to stop here would be to ignore the dimensions along which these approaches may be followed. Each of these research agendas may be pursued along the dimensions of time and space. In other words, legal research under these headings can be enriched by looking back into the past to see how things have changed through time, or by looking across at other countries or jurisdictions to see how things happen elsewhere. For this reason, this book concludes with chapters on historical and comparative legal research.

It is important for students of law to recognise that different approaches to its study exist and that they involve different research methods. Each approach to the study of law tends to ask its own kind of question and use it own kind of method. Students need to be able to recognise the difference between, for example, an empirical and a philosophical question, or between an historical and comparative question. Crucially, you need to be able to recognise that the research questions which are characteristic of one approach cannot generally be answered with the method of another. For example, empirical questions cannot be answered through philosophical methods. Comparative questions cannot be answered with historical methods, and so forth.

I must conclude this introduction, however, by stressing that this "map" is simply a device to help you understand the terrain of modern legal scholarship. Typologies—lists of types—are usually most useful when not treated too dogmatically. As with many systems of categorisation, the real world is a little messier than the abstract categories which seek to capture it. The types of legal scholarship set out here are meant to be illustrative rather than restrictive. It must be stressed that there is a degree of overlap between the categories of legal scholarship that we describe. For example, empirical scholarship can provide grounds for critical work on law, and critical scholarship can set out an agenda of questions for empirical investigation. Equally, philosophical work can animate and inform doctrinal work. Conversely, doctrinal work can contribute to philosophical debates. Popular cultural work can speak to debates within critical and empirical scholarship. And as we pointed out above, historical research and comparative scholarship can enrich all five of the main research agendas

Nonetheless, as a general guiding device—particularly in your opening encounters with legal study—we think this "map" is useful in terms of setting out the main forms of scholarship that you will come across in your studies. It is meant to help organise your thinking at the beginning of your studies. It is a platform from which you can begin your voyage of legal enquiry. You will probably find that, as your knowledge deepens, you will be able to find a degree of fault with it. That is a good thing. It will show learning and critical thinking. However, one needs a starting point, even though it may have imperfections: this book is offered as a useful and helpful starting point.

---

[i]   This phrase was first used by David Downes to describe criminology: see Paul Rock, The History of Criminology (Aldershot: Dartmouth, 1994), p.xii.

# 1. DOCTRINAL APPROACHES

*Jenny Steele*

INTRODUCTION: WHAT IS DOCTRINAL STUDY?

"Doctrinal study" still forms the core of every undergraduate law degree, and it continues to be the most widespread form of legal study, even when mixed with other approaches. Indeed, skill in doctrinal method could be said to be what distinguishes the lawyer from the non-lawyer. This chapter will say something about what is involved in doctrinal study of law, its achievements, its breadth, and its potential. But it will also reflect on challenges to doctrinal method and its place at the heart of legal study, and the kind of response that these challenges have provoked—when they have provoked a response—from predominantly doctrinal lawyers.

First though, the very idea of "doctrinal" study requires some explanation. The word "doctrinal" is in many ways unsatisfactory. It is generally now chosen above the alternative description of "black letter" law, which can be thought too dismissive. The epithet "black letter" could be taken to refer to a particular (rather stuffy) corner within the realms of doctrinal study. To describe an approach as "black letter" might imply that it accounts only for the letter of the law as written in the books, that it does not engage much in interpretation or creative thinking, and that it struggles to envisage evaluative questions about the law. None of this describes what "doctrinal" study of law is generally about. But arguably, the description "doctrinal" is also unsatisfactory, and has been settled on only for lack of a better alternative.

Outside the law, "doctrine" is generally associated with specific and possibly dogmatic teachings to be absorbed, learned, and not questioned—hence its extension, "doctrinaire", to capture an unyielding and unreasoning position and, worse, the idea of "indoctrination" into particular ideas which cannot be questioned. Fortunately, this is by no means what lawyers mean by "doctrinal" study. Doctrinal study is not concerned with learning a few clear rules which are then to be applied come what may. Nor is higher level doctrinal study about learning all of the applicable rules together with all of the applicable exceptions. To be sure, a doctrinal lawyer will set considerable store by a sound knowledge base. But beyond this, argument, reasoning, disagreement, and persuasion are all important elements of "doctrinal" approaches in law; and it is understood that areas of uncertainty will often—possibly always—be encountered where these skills can and must be deployed.

"Doctrinal" study is concerned with the substantive content of the law, and therefore with the analysis of legal materials, primarily cases and statutes, and primarily for the kinds of purposes associated with lawyering (identification of the legal position; resolution of potential or actual questions relating to parties' rights and liabilities; identification of gaps in the law that require reform or features of it that can be improved). In the course of this, the materials are interpreted, manipulated, tested and developed. In some areas of the law, which are relatively new or have had less attention, the most important aspect of doctrinal work may be that a mass of material is clearly explained and its overall shape articulated in a helpful way. If the shape arrived at can be criticised, it does not undermine the achievement of having presented something capable of critical response in the first place.

It should be a relief to all those approaching law for the first time that doctrinal study is emphatically not merely about absorbing information or facts, though plenty of information must be absorbed and processed. Less of a relief perhaps is that while it is generally agreed that there is no one right answer to most legal questions, there are abundant potential ways of getting the answer wrong, through false or missing information, flawed reasoning, or implausible analogy—or simply by not thinking of the "issues" that a lawyer would think might arise. Doctrinal study is closely associated with legal expertise, and with "thinking like a lawyer", and this is both its strength and its weakness. To engage in doctrinal analysis is to get involved in legal argument, or at least to appreciate what legal protagonists (including reformers) are, and were, doing when the content of the law is or was being interpreted and developed. Those who are experienced in doctrinal method will also understand why it is exceedingly difficult to predict what the impact of any attempt to state or change the law might ultimately be. And while doctrinal analysis may be engaged in for a broader range of purposes than the ones identified already, it always means engaging "like a lawyer", or even as a lawyer. While doctrinal study is the most traditional approach to the study of law, this does not mean that it has not moved on nor that it is dull or unrewarding. Indeed, it will be suggested in this chapter that the degree to which doctrinal approaches can adapt and move on has sometimes been under-appreciated. It is easy to criticise a simplified model of doctrinal method, and to overlook the potential richness and diversity that may be involved.

## DOCTRINAL METHOD AND LEGAL PRACTICE

Having said all of this, it might be argued that doctrinal study boils down to no more than professional competence, and that this forms the common denominator for all doctrinal approaches. And in truth, most lawyers do not spend nearly as much time reflecting on the nature of their methods as just getting on with it (and requiring students to become adept at doing it too). This may well be a legacy of the way the study of law in our jurisdictions, but particularly the common law part, arose only gradually and a great deal later than the practice of law. Legal methods were forged, and learned, by doing law, or transmitted at the Inns of Court, and only belatedly moved into the universities.

This was a particular issue for English "common law".[1]  In England, when William Blackstone was appointed to the Vinerian Chair in Law at the University of Oxford in 1758, his became the first university Chair devoted to the study of common law. (Scotland, which is a part of the civil law family, did better: Edinburgh had its first professor of Public Law and the Law of Nature and Nations in 1707, and no fewer than four law professors by 1722.) Prior to this, universities taught only ecclesiastical law and Roman law, and common law was taught only practically, at the Inns of Court. Even then, Blackstone still did not have any students of English law. It might be sensed that where the career of common law in the universities was concerned, there was a felt deficiency to be made up from the start. Blackstone himself argued that throughout Europe, people thought some understanding of the law an essential aspect of their education—perhaps because the law was presented in civilian codes in the form of simple and abstract statements easily identified as statements of rights and obligations. In common law, the simplest statement of law has to be derived from the decisions of numerous courts and legislatures and is in some sense a generalisation, an interpretation, not based simply on words or individual texts. To some extent, the simpler the statement, the harder one has to dig to get it. What we now call "doctrinal" propositions (statements of the substance of the law) have, in this sense, to be built from the ground up. As Blackstone put it

> "… it has been the peculiar lot of our admirable system of laws, to be neglected, and even unknown, by all but one practical profession; though built upon the soundest foundations, and approved by the experience of ages."[2]

Study of common law always had a lot of catching up to do. Its virtues were practical and pragmatic; and it is not surprising if Blackstone and others sometimes wanted to show that it embodied other higher order values in order to promote the cause. Academic common lawyers, once there were some, had a great deal of doctrinal groundwork to do to gain acceptance for their subject.

The issue of law's practicality has therefore been present throughout its career in the universities. Today, the link between doctrinal law, and legal practice, continues to be the focus for many arguments both for and against the value of doctrinal approaches. It is sometimes suggested that thanks to the dominance of doctrinal approaches, academic law is typically a "parasitic" subject—parasitic, that is, on practice.[3]  This is a very loaded way of expressing the relationship. It is argued in reply that academic law loses its value as it moves away from the concerns of practice. This sort of tension was referred to light-heartedly by Stephen Sedley, a former Court of Appeal Judge, when he drew analogies between law, and "plumbing".[4]  As we all know, working plumbing is a necessary feature of any modern habitation. The deeper point being made is that the study of law is not at its best when it gets above its practical station, and like good plumbers, virtuoso doctrinal lawyers are simply too sought-after to stop and wonder whether their skills are worthwhile. But built into the reference to plumbing is also a perception that other approaches tend to look down upon the exercise of doctrinal study (and some more theoretically inclined doctrinal lawyers look down upon the practical branch). One of the questions to be addressed is whether doctrinal lawyers are *merely* plumbers, to be contrasted with the more complex (perhaps) and self-conscious (certainly) activities of some of the other approaches explored in this book.

To make matters worse for doctrinal approaches, the argument that doctrinal study is limited and parasitic, merely an expression of professional competence, is not the only challenge it faces. As you will see in Chapter 4, numerous critical approaches have gone further than this, and used the supposed "neutrality" of law (and of lawyers' skills) as a starting point for their own critique of what they call "liberal legalism". On this account, expertise and supposed neutrality are a smokescreen for hidden values, and possibly even a tool of oppression. To some extent, doctrinal approaches have a difficult corner to fight. They can maintain that they are primarily practical and removed from other more normative debates about law, so that they do not operate to provide a "perspective" at all; they can supplement their approach and connect with other perspectives, arguing that the right people to write about law really are those who are legally trained; or they can develop normative arguments to explain why it is right and appropriate for lawyers to stick to what lawyers do—a normative defence of formal skills, and liberal legalism. Over the course of this chapter, we will think about these possibilities.

## THE INDISPENSABLE NATURE OF DOCTRINAL APPROACHES

Ability to engage at a "doctrinal" level is a necessary element of the effective study of law. For one thing, even to understand the provisions of the law, there is a need for analysis and interpretation. No single reading of a vast amount of material will give a reliable sense of how the law stands, and lawyers depend on synthesising not only this primary material, but also the information and interpretation of others. The work of doctrinal lawyers has been needed even to suggest what categories should be used in interpreting and understanding the law. For example, Blackstone's *Commentaries on the Laws of England* (published in 1765–1769) divided its exploration of the law into blocks such as rights of persons and rights of things; private wrongs and public wrongs. Cases and even statutes alone are not inclined to do this. Oddly enough, studies such as this have been criticised for giving a false impression of order and coherence in the law. This is a familiar thread in critical responses to doctrinal law—that they falsely present as orderly that which is chaotic. But attempts to systematise and to comprehend are necessary starting points, and capable in turn of having an impact on the way that law in practice is ordered, understood, and developed. Systematisation does not necessarily entail seeing boundaries as rigid and absolute, though it can of course be used to that end. The point is that to see them as flexible is not a departure from doctrinal method.

Beyond this, to understand law as a phenomenon requires at least a degree of understanding of what its participants are doing, and how they are working. To study law without studying doctrinal method could be understood to be like studying only its outer shell. The nature of legal reasoning is as important as the "rules" or principles applied.

At a very simple level, it would be difficult to make a difference to law and its study without being able to keep pace with its internal arguments. The facility with which lawyers continue to move in and out of the universities and the profession illustrates that university lawyers are deploying skills which are of use at the higher levels of professional law, and makes questionable the idea that academic law is merely "parasitic". There are various law journals where readers and contributors are a mixture of academics and practitioners, and academic work is often cited in the course of judgments. At the top of the scale, academic lawyers have often been involved in senior roles in law reform bodies. And in many countries—including to a greater extent than before the United Kingdom— academics have been able to move into judicial roles (and vice versa). This reflects the more general fact that academic doctrinal lawyers are participants in the development of the law. The job of understanding the law is never done, because it develops on a daily basis whether through deliberate reform and creation of new law, or through the resolution of disputes or actions of various sorts. At each stage, there is argument, and through the resolution of arguments put in respect of practical law-making and practical disputes, the law moves and must be analysed again.

POTENTIAL

As we have just pointed out, the work of the doctrinal lawyer is never done. For those who enjoy doctrinal study, the good news is that there is no practical need to move on. The huge mass of legal material is unlikely to be simplified. There are always new developments, new understandings to be elaborated, and even areas of law which have remained under-explored. This may happen because they are outside the confines of the "core curriculum", and most particularly if they are complex and closely connected to practice, since the rewards for those who move out of the university and into the profession are likely to be greater. Equally, new areas (like information technology law, or before that competition law) will continue to emerge which require skilled doctrinal interpreters, but also invite the development of some underpinning debate and the identification of shared concerns. A familiar criticism of doctrinal method is that it purports to be "value free". Though the skills imparted to law students may not appear to emphasise substantive values, the idea that doctrinal lawyers actively purport to be "value free" is not supported by looking at the debates between academics. In some areas, like environmental law, or health care law, discussion of values is very much part of the emergence and delineation of the field of study. In the second of these cases, the very name of the subject has been debated in line with the search for what matters most about it: should it be seen in terms of medical law; medical law and ethics, or health care law? Doctrinal lawyers of a broader or narrower frame of mind are therefore inherently involved in the definition of areas of law and, nowadays, of the concerns which are thought to animate them, and this may be more or less explicit. Turning to a new area of law and trying to understand it is not only about learning doctrinal detail, but also about understanding what issues matter to its participants, and what fault lines divide them. Loving the law is not necessarily the sign of an uncritical mind. In addition to the sheer scale of the law and its inherent tendency to replicate itself further, there is a very broad range of work awaiting the doctrinal lawyer.

As we have seen, doctrinal lawyers have been the systematisers of the law. It may appear that this kind of work is now largely completed, but that is not quite the case. A recent example is the development of accounts of an English law of "unjust enrichment", largely through the work of academics (and academic-practitioners) working with relatively limited English legal materials, but with the assistance of comparative study (drawing, for example, on the examples of US and German law). This has ultimately had a noticeable impact on the decisions of the highest courts, sometimes determining the destination of multi-million pound funds, and shows that new rationalisations of the law can still be developed. Much more generally, doctrinal lawyers are regularly involved in the exercise of identifying and extracting principles, policies, patterns, and objectives in the law, with a view to seeing the wood for the trees, even if this can only rarely enable them to find whole new subjects or threads in the law. Nevertheless, most doctrinal lawyers are engaged in thinking purposively; thinking as lawyers think; and therefore, at some level, in attempting to influence the shape of the law or its understanding—and, of course, in arguing about it. One of the more rewarding exercises in doctrinal scholarship is returning to a source which lawyers believe is understood, and finding that it can be reinterpreted to very different effect. Some such sources are returned to time and again, almost like biblical texts, and interpreted afresh. Others don't attract the same attention. The work is always there to be done. And this, to some extent, is why a number of other disciplines find law such a tempting target. It is an endless source of real examples. The point is that the territory is not empty of academic inhabitants: the land is already occupied, and we should expect a few territorial battles.

## LIMITATIONS

It is time to accept, however, that there are downsides to thinking like a lawyer and operating within the law. This may begin to operate as a restriction on the questions that can be asked, let alone the answers that can be given. This is a limitation which may be felt by any thoughtful lawyer, and there is a range of possible responses to it. But it has also, as we have begun to see, been one of the factors making doctrinal approaches the target of critique by others. In the rest of this section, we reflect on some such questions.

First, the ability to handle legal material has its own limits. Tacitly or not, a doctrinal lawyer who ventures into *evaluation* of the law will at some, hard to define point step outside doctrinal analysis in order to do so. There may be an exception where consistency is concerned, since this is a cherished part of the method itself. Beyond this even common criteria such as "clarity" are evaluative and imply some virtue which is not explained by the exercise of interpretation, though it may be implied by other lawyerly skills such as *experience*. This is not always clearly recognised. Law articles regularly urge one change or interpretation above another, and not merely on the basis of consistency. Arguments are put that extending remedies would be more fair and just, and the idea that the job of the law is to do justice or that fairness consists in holding wrongdoers to account (rather than, say, distributing risks of misfortune) is not always spelled out. For all these reasons, skilled doctrinal lawyers have themselves often looked to public policy discussions; empirical evidence; historical analysis, and other sources, to extend the boundaries of analysis. There is no inherent reason why doctrinal analysis and other approaches should not be mixed. Indeed there is every reason why they should be, and a tradition of mixing the two made some inroads in the 1970s, developing into a movement loosely described as the "law in context" movement. Although this extension of boundaries has caused friction (who wants to be defined as studying a practical subject *out* of context?), there is every reason why doctrinal lawyers should be involved as key participants in this type of work.

Some doctrinal lawyers have asked broader questions about their own methods. For example, they have explored the openness of legal thinking to changing currents of opinion, and tried to articulate with a degree of precision how this might come about. Why leave historical analysis of law, for example, to the non-lawyers? Doctrinal lawyers should be involved in analysis of influences on the body of law with which they deal—a point made by the legal historian S.F.C. Milsom, who thought some of his historically trained colleagues were inclined to miss certain features of the material they were analysing, by *not* thinking like a lawyer.[5] This is an interesting perspective, since he was speaking primarily of the medieval period, implying a great deal of continuity in what lawyers might think and try to achieve even while studying the process of legal change. Yet exercises in exactly this sort of hybrid scholarship have raised hackles and been perceived as threatening to the exercise of doctrinal scholarship itself, primarily because they question the core importance of "coherence" within the law. How can law be "coherent" if it is also susceptible to change in accord with its times? This sort of argument reappears in many contexts and is to some extent a question about doctrinal method. To what extent is law a closed and expert system, within the boundaries of a community of doctrinal expertise? To what extent is it open to outside influences, and in what ways? How, in other words, does a process of change actually operate within a system like law, where older decisions have particular and enduring significance?

This connects to a much more general question, which is the extent to which doctrinal lawyers might fail to see the overall shape of the edifice of law, in much the same way that scholars looking only at its outer structure fail to understand some key features of its nature. To some extent, this is about a propensity not to consider empirical questions. Through their very connection with practice, doctrinal scholars may simply continue to do, and see, that which is familiar to them. This is the sort of phenomenon illustrated by classic "gap" studies, identifying the space between law in practice, and law in the books. In the area of tort liability, for example, enormous amounts of doctrinal effort are poured into analysis of the circumstances in which a "duty of care" is owed by one party to another. This question is represented in the higher courts and in textbooks (including one written by this author) and journal discussion. Yet only a handful of cases each year in England and Wales raise such questions in court. Thousands of others are resolved without having to consider such questions, without going to court, and increasingly, without the necessity of consulting lawyers rather than other negotiators. These are "routine" cases, where the primary questions concern quantum—how much money will actually be paid? Is it really true to say that doctrinal lawyers understand the nature of law, just because they are among its protagonists, and share a common language with the profession? Naturally, the solution is for doctrinal lawyers to supplement their understanding by reading such studies and taking them into account in their model of what law is, and one hopes that law reform proceeds on precisely this basis. Equally naturally, such a suggestion would not necessarily be universally welcomed.

Another potentially powerful argument against doctrinal approaches claims that despite their link with the professional practice of law, they are primarily concerned not with "life" but with "text". A great deal of doctrinal work is, as we have seen, involved in interpretation of, broadly, legal texts, and with the production of an evaluative response. We have already touched on the problem that not all law is about texts, and that the texts won't offer guidance on the true shape and scale of the law in operation. Associated with this is a move to reunite legal study with practice in a critically aware fashion. For example, some law schools choose to educate students partly through experience of clinical work, emphasising "law in action" as much as "law in the books". This movement is, therefore, *more* practical than doctrinal approaches, rather in defiance of the criticism that the study of law is too closely associated with the profession; and seeks to reunite legal study with life (and law), not (simply) with text.

In the association of doctrinal approaches with examination of "texts", we also encounter a new challenge. How to understand the process of reading texts is of course the subject of a significant thread of post-modernist critique. Arguably, doctrinal lawyers are right not to be overly concerned about this challenge. Whilst post-modernist critique based on contingency, lack of clear meaning, and relativity of truth, may have lessons for those studying law and will operate as a reminder of what is involved in selecting an interpretation, most doctrinal lawyers may answer quite tetchily that they are well aware of these issues already and indeed deal with them on a daily basis. But they choose to get on with the exercise of interpretation rather than to stop to point out what it involves.

It is, however, quite possible to imagine a much more reflective, critical, or "post-modernist" strand within doctrinal study of law. In fact, such a strand arguably exists quite strongly at present. For example, a recent *Feminist Judgments* project collected a number of rewritten judgments, based on real decisions of the higher courts, and framed from a range of feminist points of view.[6] This is a fascinating exercise not only in feminist method, but also in the potential of legal doctrinal approaches. The reasoned judgment could be taken to be the very paradigm of doctrinal law, pulling together legal sources and attempting to achieve sound results while also achieving a sense of authority. The project goes beyond earlier attempts to suggest that this process, and the sense of authority itself, are merely a "cloak". In attempting to *write* judgments, the participants had to decide which aspects of judgment-writing were to be embraced, and which rejected. It can be seen that certain features of the typical legal judgment were subverted or changed in the process. In particular, the writers typically chose to use the names of protagonists, humanizing them rather than treating them in terms of their abstract relations. This means that many elements of the context of the case were included in consideration, which might have been submerged in legal argument. The judgments illustrate that selection of "relevant" material can be decisive, and political, yet at the same time, they demonstrate that doctrinal analysis does not collapse under the weight of this recognition. Other aspects of judgment, thought of as required for any claim to authority, were deliberately left intact. In particular, the judgments seek to express justifications which are consistent with legal principles, and to achieve results which can be applied in other relevant cases. They do not proceed, for example, on the simple basis that results should be reached which are best for women, or for the less powerful party. The overriding point is that this exercise proved to be quite possible. Doctrinal study is a malleable exercise, and survives a great deal of "uncloaking" of its methods.

## BOUNDARIES

Law is a complex and significant social phenomenon and it is not surprising that scholars from a number of disciplines have wanted to analyse it—or parts of it—in their own way. We have already mentioned in passing the potential for empirical, comparative, and historical perspectives (for example) to broaden the horizons of lawyers and render doctrinal analysis one element in a broader understanding of the law. These are further explored in later chapters. Another intruder is economics. Largely in the United States, scholars trained in a particular form of economic analysis have insisted that common law, in particular, embodies a tendency to evolve towards efficient outcomes, and that this is the true explanation of the underlying doctrines of the common law—even if courts have not expressed them to have these functions. In the United Kingdom, resistance to this attempt to reinterpret legal discourse and explain it in very specific functional terms has been instrumental in the creation of a new "internalism" in doctrinal scholarship: against the trend of all the other developments above, some have argued for the barriers of doctrinal study to be reinforced—with philosophy on the inside of the barriers.

As we will see in Chapter 2, there has been a long tradition of partnership between philosophy and law. As just one example, the link between legal and moral values, or their separation, is one of the longest standing of theoretical questions about the law. Equally, doctrinal approaches, as we have seen, have felt the force of some quite determined critique from a number of different angles. Doctrinal study has been described as valueless, or as pedalling hidden values; it has been described both as overly parasitic on practice and overly fixated on texts; objective judgment has been determined to be impossible; and an economic reinterpretation of legal rules has been undertaken to discover an underlying purpose of which lawyers themselves were unaware. It is not surprising that many doctrinal lawyers have been ready to accept the sort of life-line that some philosopher lawyers appear to be able to offer, giving new weight to the existing practice of just getting on with law. A relatively new trend can be discerned, of seeking normative, philosophical arguments in favour of the very closure which is criticised by other approaches. This amounts to a decision to close the boundaries and move inward to study law's doctrines in an increasingly abstract way, while making a virtue of it. Unfortunately, this can lead to new border skirmishes, between philosophically-inclined doctrinal lawyers, and those more open to the extension of the discipline to empirical, historical, or contextual study.

## CONCLUDING THOUGHTS

The doctrinal tradition is the longest established aspect of the study of our system of law. In the early days of legal study, doctrinal approaches were indispensable to the definition of the subject. They remain indispensable today. Waves of challengers have to one extent or another been absorbed, or repelled, and the consequence is a rather richer and more varied body of doctrinal scholarship than its critics would have us believe. Incorporating the more pertinent features of critique means being willing to supplement doctrinal method, and to be aware of its nature and its limits. There are doctrinal scholars who embrace what this means for the practice of doctrinal law, others who resist it, and still others who take no notice. Above all, none of the supplementary or hostile approaches can lead us to abandon doctrinal approaches altogether. Not only are such approaches core to the academic study of law, they have come to represent lawyerly skills. Unlike the other approaches explored in this book, they therefore form part of the subject to be studied (and criticised).

FURTHER READING

Bartie, Susan, "The Lingering Core of Legal Scholarship" (2010) 30 *Legal Studies* 345.

Feldman, David, "The Nature of Legal Scholarship" (1989) 52 *Modern Law Review* 498.

Rubin, Edward L., "The Practice and Discourse of Legal Scholarship" (1988) 86 *Michigan Law Review* 1835.

Sugarman, David, "Legal Theory, the Common Law Mind and the Making of the Textbook Tradition", in W. Twining (ed), *Legal Theory and the Common Law* (Oxford: Oxford University Press, 1986).

Twining, William, *Blackstone's Tower: The English Law School* (London: Sweet and Maxwell, 1994).

---

[1] Differences between civil law and common law are outlined in Chapter 7, on Comparative Approaches.

[2] W. Blackstone, *Commentaries on the Laws of England*, Introduction, Part the First, "On the Study of Law", at 5. This was read in Oxford at the opening of the Vinerian lectures, in 1758.

[3] W.T. Murphy and S. Roberts, "Introduction" (1987) 50 M.L.R. 677. The collection of essays being introduced was concerned with legal scholarship in the common law world.

[4] S. Sedley, "Law and Plumbing" (2008) 28 L.S. 629.

[5] S.F.C. Milsom, *A Natural History of the Common Law* (2003, Columbia University Press).

[6] R. Hunter, C. McGlynn, E. Rackley (eds), *Feminist Judgments: From Theory to Practice* (Hart Publishing, 2010). This includes a very interesting foreword from Brenda Hale, the only woman so far to sit as a member of the UK's highest court.

---

## 2. LAW AND PHILOSOPHY

*John Gardner*

WHAT IS PHILOSOPHY?

"BMW's design philosophy is based around authenticity: we want our car design to express what you experience when you drive our vehicles."[1]

"Our philosophy is to use what is good from the past to create a future which is better."[2]

"Free Cone Day reinforces the Ben and Jerry's philosophy of giving back to the community."[3]

"Our Philosophy ... You can make money without doing evil ... Great just isn't good enough ... [etc., etc.]."[4]

If you search for "our philosophy" on the web you will find an amazing range of organisations, from estate agents to waste-disposal contractors to animal hospitals, claiming philosophies for themselves. A philosophy in this sense is a set of goals or maxims, usually the most general (and sometimes the most vacuous) ones that an organisation can muster to cheerlead itself with. Some law students seem to expect their excursions into the philosophy of law to offer them something similar for law. "Our philosophy of law: Access to justice for all!" "Our philosophy of law: Strict construction of statutes!" Those with such hopes are doomed to be disappointed. The connection between feel-good catchphrases and political slogans on the one hand, and philosophy as an academic discipline on the other, is very remote indeed. Philosophical theses are rarely goals or maxims (although they may be theses *about* goals and maxims). Moreover, it is very rare for trained philosophers to profess that they have such a grand thing as "a philosophy". Those who rashly do so, perhaps in a late-career interview reflecting on a lifetime's achievements, are typically viewed with suspicion or pity by their colleagues. Why? Philosophy is not primarily a product but an activity, and those who engage in it, although occasionally interested in making sense of big sweeping mantras that fill the human heart with wonder, tend to be more widely occupied with exact and difficult theses that fill the human mind with distinctions.

That, at any rate, is the modus operandi of the "analytical" philosophers that have come to dominate the English-language version of the discipline. They are "analytical" because they like to analyse, breaking every apparently big question down into small, and sometimes apparently disconnected, sub-questions. There is also a long tradition of "synthetical" philosophy, growing mainly out of the German Enlightenment, but nowadays more closely associated with *les grands philosophes* that populate late-night French TV. They like to synthesise, showing how many small and apparently disconnected questions can be folded into one big question. The synthesists tend to have more to offer to those who like to have their hearts filled with wonder. That may (or may not) be what the marketeers of the skincare brand Philosophy are trying to tap into when they write, bizarrely: "philosophy: to believe is to perceive the miraculous".[5]

In this chapter I will not invite you to perceive any miracles, let alone to read such a perception into all of your beliefs. To begin with: believing is not a kind of perceiving, whether of miracles or otherwise. Perception is a possible way of coming to believe, and belief, reciprocally, can alter perception. As these pernickety remarks about a dumb example of sales gibberish give away, I was trained in the analytical school of philosophy myself, which left me with a particular allergy to hogwash of the type associated with skincare marketing, feng shui, and self-help books. The analytical way, not surprisingly, is the way of doing philosophy that I will mainly be telling you about.

But let me start with a classical, etymologically pure explanation of what philosophy is, one that ought to appeal to analysts and synthesists alike. Philosophy is the love (*philos*) of wisdom (*sophia*). Both parts of the name matter. First let me tell you what kind of love, then what kind of wisdom.

## Feel the love

Karl Marx once famously wrote: "Philosophers have hitherto only understood the world in various ways; the point is to transform it."[6] Those are not the words of somebody with a very philosophical temperament. Philosophers, like astronomers, aim at understanding. Sometimes their ideas, like those of astronomers, may catch on and even have transformative effects on civilizations. But those effects are not what they pursue as philosophers. If you want to see why, just consider the case of Marx himself. His efforts to transform the world were in large measure cataclysmic, even in their own terms. Marx was way out of his depths as an agitator for revolution and left a shocking legacy of human misery and oppression behind him. Ultimately, in a bitter irony, the collapse from within of the alternative economic system that he naively inspired helped to prop up the ideology of unbridled capitalism that he rightly despised, and that means a new world of misery and oppression in this century (think credit crunch, war on terror, etc.) that may come to equal the misery and oppression meted out by Marx's supposed followers in the last. So Marx's record as a world-changer is far from distinguished. When he restricted himself to merely understanding the world, however, Marx did a truly first-rate job. If you love wisdom, you should read *Kapital*.[7] By an accumulation of insights it transforms the way one sees the human condition. Perhaps you could follow in these great philosophical footsteps? If you would like to transform anything other than understanding, however, you should probably abandon philosophy for another line of work.

Maybe you could become a lawyer instead? As a lawyer you could achieve all sorts of further things by *using* your understanding. As a barrister or solicitor, for example, you could use what you have learnt at law school to give advice to people in trouble, to plan and execute novel transactions, to negotiate and mediate in disputes, or to represent people in court. Later, you might become the kind of judge who, on occasions, actually gets to settle what the law is in the course of applying it. As a Law Commissioner or legal academic, meanwhile, you might help to shape the law in a different way, by influencing its development or reform. You should not be too optimistic about the scale of the changes you will help to bring about in the course of your legal career. Nor should you assume that they will all, or even mostly, be for the best (like Marx you will have to dice with unintended consequences). Nevertheless, as a lawyer you might well seek understanding mainly in order to do something else with it. Legal understanding is there, ultimately, to be put to further use, and that is because the law itself is there, ultimately, to be put to further use. Lawyers, even academic lawyers, are for this reason and in this sense practically-minded people. They want to see things done. No wonder, then, that they often find philosophers bewildering. A typical philosopher *just wants to understand*; or, in more outward-looking moments, *just wants to add to the stock of human understanding*. That is what is meant by their *love* of wisdom. It is not the mere pursuit of wisdom. It is the pursuit of wisdom for its own sake, without much regard to the strange and even perverse uses to which others, such as lawyers, politicians, priests, and marketeers, might put it.

### A word to the wise

But which wisdom? This is a bit harder to explain. I have spoken so far of "understanding" but that word points to nothing special about philosophy. Mathematicians and psychologists and paleontologists and academic linguists and academic lawyers are also trying to understand things (whether just for the sake of understanding or otherwise). These other disciplines can be distinguished from each other mainly by *what* they are trying to understand. Most academic disciplines are defined by a subject-matter. Historians study the past, chemists study chemicals, demographers study populations, sociologists study social forms and trends, academic lawyers study legal doctrine, psychologists study the mind. So which subject-matter, we might ask, is the distinctive one studied by philosophers? Nothing, it seems, that belongs on the same list. Philosophers can find things to study in any of the above subject-matters, and so can raise philosophical questions bearing on each of the above disciplines. There are also philosophical questions relating to (and sometimes addressed within) astronomy, anthropology, virology, physiology, geography, and psychology. Indeed whole branches of philosophy (philosophy of law, philosophy of physics, philosophy of social science, philosophy of maths, philosophy of psychology, etc.) have coalesced around the philosophical questions raised by the subject-matters of other disciplines.

One conclusion you could reasonably draw is that philosophy is defined not by its subject-matter, which includes absolutely everything, but by the kind of questions it asks about whatever subject-matter it engages with. Another (philosopher's) way to put the suggestion, and in the process to add more substance to it, is to say that philosophy has a *second-order* subject-matter. Physicists and historians ask (first-order) questions about particular subject-matters, respectively physical and historical events and processes. Philosophers ask (second-order) questions thrown up by those (first-order) questions, such as: "What is an event? How does it differ from a process? Is the physical world the only world? Could history have been otherwise?" Indeed some philosophers keep going in a vaguely Monty Python way. Some of them go on to ask (third-order) questions about the (second-order) questions that they ask about the (first-order) questions encountered by other disciplines: "What kind of question", they ask, "is 'What is an event?'?" Not surprisingly, philosophers who head this way are often the butt of jokes about disappearing into their own orifices. In the trade, their questions are known as meta-philosophy (or "philosophy of philosophy") ones. They subject philosophy itself to the kind of interrogation to which philosophy is always subjecting everything else.

If you want a good example of a philosophical question, there is no better place to start than with what some think of as the hard core of philosophy, a specialism known as "ontology". Ontologists ask: What are the most elementary building blocks of reality? You may think that this question is the same one that has long been pursued in the natural sciences, especially in particle physics. We once thought fire, earth, water; later atoms; now we have worked our way down, by observation and postulation, to quarks and bosons. But "quarks and bosons" is no answer, not even a possible answer, to the question that is posed by ontology. Physicists assume, normally without argument, that "reality" (in the question "What are reality's elementary building blocks?") means physical reality. That is the specialised reality they are trained to understand, in the same way that lawyers are trained to understand legal reality and sociologists are trained to understand social reality. Philosophers, by contrast, are trained to ask whether the specialised reality of physics (or of law, sociology, etc.) is the whole of reality, or even an irreducible part of it. That, you will notice, is a second-order question: a further "building blocks" question about the original "building blocks" question as other disciplines, like physics, might ask it.

Ontologists contribute to answering this second-order question by distinguishing among, and establishing the relationships between, such things as entities, properties, events, states of affairs, processes, and facts. These categories (unlike those of quark and boson) are not the special preserve of natural scientists, and do not steer us automatically towards a physical interpretation of the world. Living creatures and rights are also entities; deaths and weddings are events; dying and negotiating are processes. These examples already hint at possible ontological questions: Do all events involve entities, as death involves living creatures? Are processes just successions of events, as might be suggested by thinking of death as a final event in the process of dying? No amount of new work in physics, law, or sociology—unless it veered into philosophical work—could answer these questions, because they concern the building blocks of all thought, and hence pertain equally to the foundations (or "presuppositions") of all of these disciplines at once.

Not all philosophers, of course, are primarily ontologists (although all are expected to be aware of what are called their "ontological commitments"). Ontology is usually regarded as a core part of a wider philosophical specialism known as "metaphysics". Non-philosophers sometimes use "metaphysical" as a term of abuse. I am not sure why. Metaphysics is the study of the presuppositions of all thought, including but not limited to, practical thought. Classic metaphysical questions include: What is causation (the very idea of it)? What is time (the very idea of it)? What is a person (the very idea of it)? And how do these ideas relate? Can persons somehow break loose from causation (by "free will" or otherwise)? Do persons preserve their identity over time? If you do not think that these questions are important, then that probably means that you are not cut out to be a philosopher; you may love wisdom but not *this* kind of wisdom. But this time it may also suggest that you are not cut out to be a lawyer either, since the law in a mature legal system constantly grapples with questions about the nature of causation, the nature of persons, and so on. That one can practise law without being aware that one is engaging with these questions (and hence with metaphysics) only goes to show that one can practice law in many ways, including some that are decidedly unquestioning.

Metaphysics blends into all other parts of philosophy. The other parts also often blend into each other, and the divisions among them, such as they are, are mainly conventions that have emerged to chop study and research up into manageable chunks. The philosophy of mind (which explores the nature of the mental realm, including its relations with the physical, and which can also perhaps be called "metaphysics of mind") blends into philosophical psychology (which explores the differences and relationships among types of mental states), and also blends into epistemology, the philosophy of knowledge (which concerns the role that the world can and should play in our grasp of it). The philosophy of language (which explores the nature of meaning and the relationship between language and reality) blends in one direction back into the philosophy of mind, and in another direction into what might be called practical philosophy—which here does not mean philosophy *used to do things* but rather the philosophy *of doing things*. Practical philosophy includes moral, political, and legal philosophy, and concerns itself with reasons for action, norms of action, and the evaluation of action. This is where the link with philosophy of language comes in, for norms of language are also norms of action (of speaking, writing, etc.). Practical philosophy may also, in another direction, be allied with epistemology (which deals with reasons and norms relevant to belief) and in yet another direction with philosophical aesthetics (which is also concerned with evaluation, although, many would say, not primarily the evaluation of action).

The words "many would say" in this last remark reveal that the links between these various areas of philosophy can also themselves emerge as topics of philosophical debate. So, for example, there are those who disagree about whether political philosophy forms part of moral philosophy, not because they are quibbling over the syllabi for different philosophy exams, but because they disagree about the relevance of moral argument to political institutions. This shows that, while the demarcations among philosophical specialisms are largely creatures of convenience, convenience is not all that is at stake in them. Philosophers can refuse to cross lines into neighbouring parts of philosophy not because those parts are unfamiliar or somehow belong to other philosophers, but (so to speak) *on principle*: because their philosophical conclusions instruct them they should not cross that line. A philosopher may say "that's moral philosophy, not political philosophy", not as a way of sticking doggedly to her job description, but as a way of communicating a claim *in* political philosophy, namely that morality (or "ordinary" morality) doesn't apply to politics.

Thinking about moral and political philosophy may lead you to wonder whether you have now lost sight of what is distinctive about philosophical questions. Don't moral and political philosophers ask straightforward first-order questions such as: "Should the doctor turn off the life support machine?", "What kinds of discrimination should we ban?" and "Must all promises be kept?" Actually, not so much. There is a field of moral philosophy sometimes called "applied ethics" (of which "bioethics" is a well-known sub-field) which may sometimes look as if it is trying to provide much the same service in respect of moral norms that lawyers sometimes provide in respect of legal norms, namely the provision of expert advice to worried lay clients, such as doctors and policymakers, who want to be told what to do next. It is very doubtful, however, whether there can be moral experts in the way that there can be legal experts, and, even if there can, it is very doubtful whether the pool of moral philosophers should be regarded as the pool from which moral experts are to be drawn. Here as with other subjects, philosophy is the natural home of second-order questions: "How should doctors think about the question of whether to turn off the life support machine? Is it only a question of consequences?" "What is discrimination? Does it have anything to do with inequality?" "What does it mean to *keep* a promise—merely to do what was promised, or to do what was promised because it was promised?" Some possible answers to these second-order questions may, it is true, have more direct first-order implications than others. So it is true, for example, that some moral philosophers endorse very boiled down explanations of how morality is organised, according to which, say, everything comes down to one ultimate moral norm. If they are right then, armed with enough information about a given predicament, someone could in principle apply the proposed one ultimate moral norm to yield decisive advice about what to do in that predicament.

Should that someone be the philosopher herself? Philosophers may have first-order moral views like anyone else and perhaps, given the philosopher's training in working out what she thinks and working out why, they are particularly likely to be sensible views. Maybe so, although my personal experience of the moral judgment of moral philosophers, including my own moral judgment, leads me doubt it. But even granting that the moral philosopher could sometimes be a good moral adviser, the giving of that advice is mainly a philosophical footnote, given the huge amount of philosophical work that has to be done before we get to it. Why should anyone think that morality boils down to so little? Why expect so much determinacy? Why assume that the morally right thing to do is also the overall right thing to do? Why suppose that quality can be quantified? And so on.

THE SCHOOL OF ARGUMENT

I said that philosophy is an activity, and I hope that I have conveyed by my sample philosophical questions that it is a highly argumentative activity. Most of a philosopher's work consists in exhibiting relationships that hold between propositions and (more generally) ideas—inferences and connections that can be drawn or blocked. This is one feature that philosophy has notably and definitively in common with law, law understood both as an academic discipline and as a professional practice. Sadly, this commonality is only erratically reflected in the bureaucratic structure of universities. In many universities with groupings of faculties or departments, philosophy has been put in with the humanities, while law has been put in with the social sciences. Both disciplines tend to find these arranged disciplinary marriages problematic. There is certainly something humanistic about philosophy. Even the philosophy of physics, by and large, tries to locate physics in our world, a world where there are (or are claimed to be) things other than physics. Meanwhile there is clearly something social about law; many legal institutions are also social institutions, and at least some legal rules are also social rules. Nevertheless, and in spite of the robust belief among many law students that they are more in the "real world" than philosophers, legal research does not consistently or straightforwardly conform to the largely empirical research agenda of social scientists (although, as the next chapter explains, there is some significant common ground).

The empirical aspects of law are the primary concern of socio-legal studies and criminology. Much of the rest of the academic study of law, in spite of some empirical aspects, could just as well be moved into the humanities division, which is where it is largely located for the purpose of allocating government research funding in the United Kingdom. But if it were moved from social sciences into humanities, it would scarcely find more intellectual affinity with most of its new bedfellows (literature, languages, history, music, fine art) than it had with its old.

Law's intellectual techniques, mainly techniques of argument, would be most continuous with those of the philosophers, who also often feel that they are out of place among the lovers of narrative and representation who share the humanities building with them.

It might well be tempting, therefore, for the two disciplines of law and philosophy to form a breakaway union, distinct from both humanities and social sciences, a School of Argument. To call it a School of Argument is not to deny, of course, that every academic discipline lives by argument. All academics argue for a living. Nevertheless both legal and philosophical training are distinctive in being training in *argument as such*, argument as a transferable skill, argument about, frankly, any subject-matter.

This comes about in the case of philosophy directly, and the case of law indirectly. As we saw, philosophy as an academic discipline has no distinctive first-order subject-matter; any subject-matter at all can give rise to philosophical questions. By contrast, law as an academic discipline does have a distinctive first-order subject matter, namely legal doctrine and its use. However, there are no limits to the range of further subject-matters to which legal doctrine may attend,[8] so by an indirect route the lawyer shares with the philosopher the ability to turn his or her argumentative hand to anything and everything. The care of children? The benefits of opera? The purpose of income tax? The justification for war? The nature of death? The value of knowledge? Just a random selection of topics about which philosophers and lawyers alike might be called upon to argue in their professional capacities, not because they are experts on those topics, but because they are experts at arguing.

There is another, deeper commonality hidden within this one. Law students are trained not only to argue about any topic, but also to argue for any cause, no matter how unappetising. A lawyer always has to be ready to be a devil's advocate. That is not just what lawyers are paid for as practitioners. It is also an essential feature of their intellectual discipline. The extent to which, as nascent lawyers, they are expected to argue in this detached way, using premises that they personally reject, is one of the things that may lead some law students to become refugees from legal education after a year or two of law school. They find that the fun of mooting wears thin. Some of these refugees flee to philosophy courses (often available as options in a law degree) in the hope that philosophy will give more credence to their own committed views, especially on moral and political questions. They hope, perhaps, to feel less compromised.

In general, these refugees are only partially satisfied with their choice of refuge. Although it is true that moral and political philosophers enjoy more latitude to represent and defend their personal views on moral and political questions in their work than most lawyers do (even academic lawyers without clients) nevertheless much philosophical work is akin to much legal work in being more concerned with the success of arguments than with the truth of premises (except to the extent that the truth of a premise in turn depends on the success of another argument). Like much legal argument, much philosophical argument takes the following form: "Even conceding A and B, C doesn't follow." Philosophy, like law, requires one to look upon the "field of pain and death"[9] with (what some people regard as) shocking *sang-froid* or dispassion. Many moral philosophers, in particular, use hypothetical examples just as gruesome as any found on a criminal law exam (think massacre, torture, theft of organs, enslavement) and manage to turn them into illustrations of the great importance of where to close the brackets in a proposition, or of the distinction between a proviso and an exception, or of assorted problems in "moral mathematics". This can be just as alienating as anything found in a law book. Some readers of such discussions understandably don't want their opposition to war, for example, to rest on such niceties as *what exactly follows from what*, niceties which (as lawyers also know) can serve warmongers as readily as peaceniks. The dictates of logic, you will learn in our School of Argument, are not the sole preserve of the good and the true. If you simply want to stand up for the good and the true, be careful before you enrol.

Our proposed School of Argument would unite two disciplines that have very close intellectual ties, then, including a shared willingness to take potshots at attractive conclusions as well as unattractive ones. Yet serious differences between the two disciplines would surely survive their new alliance and probably give rise to some factional squabbles. I noted one difference already. Lawyers, even academic lawyers, tend to be more oriented than philosophers towards seeing their thinking put to *use* (in something other than just more thinking). This sometimes affects what qualifies as a successful argument in each of the two disciplines. However, another difference between their respective modes of argumentation is perhaps more striking and pervasive. Lawyers, including academic lawyers, argue characteristically from authority. They take a proposition of law from a statute or a case, and they use it as a premise in an argument, usually an argument to another (proposed or supposed) proposition of law. This is a rather specialised argumentative activity, in which philosophers do not for the most part care to join. Indeed if you look at any list of common philosophical fallacies, you will find "appeal to authority" (aka *argumentum ad verecundiam*) high on the list. To stand up for the truth of any proposition in a philosophical way is to defend it on its merits, not on its sources. The fact that the proposition was uttered approvingly by another philosopher—even a very famous or clever one—simply does not qualify as part of the defence. Nor does the fact that a certain argument appeared in a famous philosophy book help to show that it is a valid argument. Law students, trained to find an authority for every proposition that they rely upon, find this fact about philosophy very hard to take. Most immediately, it leads them to mess up their legal philosophy (or "jurisprudence") exam. Instead of telling us what the difference is between a legal right and a legal power, whether legal reasoning is a kind of moral reasoning, whether all legal systems include customary norms, and so forth—these being the questions asked by the examiners—many law students settle for summarising what such-and-such a philosopher said about these questions, and what such-and-such a rival philosopher said in reply, and so forth. One waits in vain for the argument, *provided by the student himself,* that shows one or both of these supposedly warring parties to have been thinking on the right or the wrong lines. This lacuna is a side-effect of the deferential character of legal education, the lawyer's "bootlicking attitude to the judges"[10] ("with the very greatest respect, my Lord, it is humbly submitted that the distinguished judge's dictum is to be read more liberally", etc.) being generalised into a bootlicking attitude to all supposed grandees as far back as Plato.

Bad jurisprudence exams are the most immediate impact on law students of their yearning for the comfort of authority and the rewards of deference. But another impact runs deeper and persists longer. Lawyers tend to be a particularly sceptical bunch, and I don't mean in a good way.[11] A good way of being sceptical, it seems to me, is being sceptical of authority. Alas legal education, as we just saw, tends not to breed this kind of scepticism. Instead it tends to breed an opposite kind of scepticism: reluctance to give credence to any proposition *except* to the extent that it is backed up by authority. A traditional lawyer's reaction to many propositions debated by philosophers, therefore, is to issue the totally deadening and point-missing challenge: "Who's to say?" Or, a minor variation on the same theme: "That's a controversial suggestion." The correct philosophical response to such challenges is usually: "Lawyer alert! Fallacy of *argumentum ad verecundiam* in progress!" This response, however, may well fall on deaf ears. Just wait until you have studied law for a couple of years and see if you can still make an argument that doesn't end up relying on authority, if only on the authority of a supposed widespread consensus. If not, ask a kindly philosophy student to remind you how.

PHILOSOPHISING ABOUT LAW

One of the biggest philosophical problems about law, perhaps the biggest, is one we have just touched on. How can authorities play the role they are supposed to play in law? How can legal arguments proceed from authoritative pronouncements? Once you are a law student you will quite possibly take this way of proceeding so much for granted that you will not be able to see any problem here. That is one reason why typical "jurisprudence" courses, in which this problem is in the foreground, can be so hard for law students to get into. They cannot believe that anyone is seriously querying what they now regard as totally normal. They cannot imagine why anyone would ask:

> How are the creation, imposition, modification, and extinction of obligations and other operations on other legal entities such as rights possible? How can such things be done?[12]

This is how the problem—what we could call *the problem of how law is possible*—was formulated by H.L.A. Hart, arguably the most influential philosopher of law of modern times, at least in the English-speaking world.

But what—asks many a law student—is the problem that Hart is getting at? Why is it a problem?

There are several ways to bring alive the problem of how law is possible, two of which were emphasised and explored by Hart in a famous book called *The Concept of Law*[13]:

1. How does anyone ever acquire the ability to make law? As lawyers, we always look for someone else who conferred the ability, someone who handed out the law-making powers. But who gave this "someone else" the powers to hand out? Someone else again, presumably. Eventually we get back to something called "the constitution", which is supposed to confer the ultimate legal powers. But how? Who made the constitution and how did *they* get the legal powers to do it? How did the whole thing ever get off the ground? "It just did" is not an answer.

2. Human beings are fallible. Anything they make, they will sometimes make badly. That includes duties and rights and powers and so on. Any duty that gets made on a human being's say-so is liable to be a dodgy duty, one that should not exist. But duties are by their nature *binding* things. How can something be both binding and dodgy? If it should not exist, how can it still be a duty? So how can law both be a business of duties and rights and powers and so on, and yet also made by fallible human beings who will at least sometimes make a pig's ear of it?

Hart made great strides with these questions but of course his solutions are still widely debated. Some of the debates, in typical philosophical style, are debates about Hart's presuppositions, the things that he took for granted. Some people doubt, for example, whether he was right to suppose that all law really is made by human beings, or at any rate right to think that it is *simply* made by human beings. Maybe the dodgy duties, the ones that shouldn't have been made, just aren't law at all? Maybe the constitution has a moral, not a simply legal, basis, so the question of how it was made gives way to the question of whether it is wise, legitimate, or morally binding? Philosophers who head off in these directions are already starting to *idealise* law. They are starting to build into their explanation of how law is possible the thought that law is a good thing. Hart thought such idealisation was too high a price to pay for a solution to the problem of how law is possible. He thought we needed to explain how law is possible in a way that left open the possibility that some legal systems are a waste of space, or at least not worthy examples. In other words he thought we should separate the problem of how law is *possible* from the problem of when law is *defensible*. Indeed he thought that tackling the first question first would allow us to move onto the second question with a clear head.

The jurisprudence courses of many law schools reflect this way of carving up our inquiries about law. They begin with what is sometimes known as "clarificatory" jurisprudence (in which we study what law is like, trying to make sense of various aspects of legal life and experience, the very nature of legal rights and duties and so on) and then they move onto what is known as "justificatory" or "evaluative" or "critical" jurisprudence (in which we discuss how law can be defended or attacked, in particular what the appropriate standards of evaluation for law are). Although pedagogically convenient, this way of dividing the subject up is also treacherous in various ways. Not least, it tends to prejudge against the idealisers, who say that what counts as law depends, at least in part, on what is defensible, so that jurisprudence is "justificatory" from the word go. I personally think that these idealisers, of whom Ronald Dworkin is the leading modern light, are quite mistaken, and that Hart was right to resist their blandishments. But I am also very aware that here, as in other parts of philosophy, the lines that we draw between our topics have philosophical implications of their own. It is not only a question of convenience, but also a philosophical question in its own right, whether the "clarificatory" questions are distinct from the "justificatory" or "evaluative" or "critical" ones.

Having said that, the division of jurisprudence courses along these Hartian lines may serve, perhaps, as a bit of a corrective to the intellectual impatience of some law students, and their associated misconceptions about what the philosophy of law is and what it is supposed to be doing for them. Some people trained (or half-trained) in the dark arts of the law are dismissive of philosophical problems and of philosophers. They are practically-minded people and they want to do practically-minded things. They don't want to know about the presuppositions of their thought or their practice unless doing so will (say) help them to win cases or help them to reform the law. Some law students wishfully re-imagine philosophy of law as the part of their curriculum in which they will be liberated from doctrine to discuss law reform proposals, to debate the merits of contentious legal rules, or more generally to discuss first-order problems in legal policy. This is a misconception. It is even a misconception about the "justificatory" or "evaluative" or "critical" part of jurisprudence. Philosophy asks second-order questions. Philosophers are not moral experts (because there are no moral experts) and so they can't tell you which laws are in need of reform any better than you can tell them. Indeed no course at university can (or should) teach you what to think about the moral and political issues of the day. The point is to teach you *how* to think about them, and indeed how to think more generally. Philosophers, fortunately, are experts on that. They think hard and rigorously for a living, keeping a particular eye out for fallacy, overstatement, and muddle in the thinking of others. That expertise is what they are supposed to be bringing to your law degree, in a way that complements the closely related and yet subtly different expertise of your law teachers.

The issues in jurisprudence, or philosophy of law, that I have mentioned so far belong to what is sometimes known as "general" jurisprudence.

General jurisprudence, which for better or worse dominates many undergraduate jurisprudence courses, raises philosophical questions about law in general. How is law possible? Is all law divided into legal systems? How come? What are the basic building blocks of all law? Rules, principles, rulings? Duties, powers, rights? How are the basic building blocks themselves to be distinguished from each other? Are they also the basic building blocks of morality? Indeed are there any "necessary connections" between law and morality? How can there be legal obligations that are not moral obligations? How can legal obligations give rise to moral obligations? Is legal reasoning a kind of moral reasoning even when its premises and conclusions are immoral? Can they be *totally* immoral? These questions straddle the divide between clarificatory and justificatory jurisprudence that I just described. But they all belong alike to general jurisprudence because they are not questions that are local to particular legal systems or traditions, or to particular areas of law that a legal system might or might not possess. These questions all arise about all legal systems—about law in general.

There are also, of course, philosophical questions lurking in particular legal systems and traditions, and in particular areas of law such as criminal law and contract law. Many philosophers of law work on these too. They work on the special features of the common law tradition, or on the idea of an unwritten constitution such as that found in the United Kingdom, or on the special features of EU legal system. They work on doctrines of legal responsibility that are specific to criminal law, or to the law of torts, or to the international law of war. They work on the differences and similarities between promising and contracting, or between entrusting things and setting up what the law calls a trust. They interrogate the idea of the person, or the idea of causation, found in (say) American legal systems or Napoleonic legal systems. They are private law theorists, or international law theorists, or constitutional law theorists. This work may seem closer to that of doctrinal lawyers than does work in general jurisprudence. That is not, or not necessarily, because it is less philosophical. It is at least partly because law is a discipline with built-in system of specialisation. Lawyers are trained in one jurisdiction rather than another, and different areas of law are authoritatively carved up by the judges or the legislature and then studied by different academic experts. Unlike philosophy the demarcations are official, built into the subject-matter of study. Special jurisprudence submits to these demarcations and allows them to shape its own second-order questions. A lot of lawyers' everyday assumptions about what they are doing for a living are thereby allowed to pass unquestioned in most kinds of special jurisprudence. Not so in general jurisprudence. General jurisprudence tends to upset or problematize the law's own demarcations and assumptions, in fact its whole worldview, which makes the subject seem unfamiliar and remote, possibly even threatening, to lawyers, law teachers, and law students.

A brilliant lawyer and legal historian recently wrote, in a somewhat cranky memoir published after his death, that "In my own long experience as a teacher and to some modest extent a practitioner of law I have never once been asked the question 'What is law?'"[14] This was meant to be a poke at Hart, and those who have followed him into the perennial problems of general jurisprudence. But why should it be thought to point to a problem for philosophers of law? Consider this analogy.

Physicists do not for the most part encounter the question of whether reality is all of it physical. For the purposes of their work they normally just assume that it is; physical reality is the only kind of reality they work on. Now along comes someone working in metaphysics who raises the question of whether reality is all of it physical. Just imagine a physicist complaining: "In my own long experience as a teacher and researcher in physics I have never once (except by you philosophers) been asked the question 'Is reality all of it physical?'" The proper response from a philosopher would surely be this: "Exactly. Your complacent disciplinary assumptions are exactly what we have been sent to challenge." Would it then be a good rejoinder for the physicist to say, as our cranky legal historian says, that the philosopher's concerns are "so unrelated to the real world as to be rubbish"?[15] No it would not, and the reason is that the question of what *counts* as the real world, what *forms part* of the real world, is exactly the question that the philosopher is raising with the physicist. No less so the philosopher of law with the lawyer. To see if law is part of the "real world" we have to find out what it really is, how it can possibly exist, and what else must exist as part of it or in tandem with it. The lawyer no less than the physicist is making philosophical assumptions about what qualifies as real. The lawyer no less than the physicist can be challenged and interrogated on those assumptions. To refuse to rise to those challenges is to embrace a kind of quietism in the face of the dominant ideology of law and legal education; it is to contribute to breeding lawyers who are skeptical in the wrong way, when one could breed lawyers who are sceptical in the right way, who can see that law's claim to authority is not only morally but also conceptually problematic, and that that law's claim to be "in the real world" therefore rests on shaky foundations.

WILL PHILOSOPHY MAKE YOU RICH?

Legal learning shades into philosophical reflection. The two subjects not only have affinities. They also have continuities. That is why the word "jurisprudence" (legal wisdom) can be used to refer to both the philosophy of law (as I have used it here) and the doctrinal thinking of the higher courts in any legal system. In spite of these affinities and continuities, many law students are alienated by their encounters with the philosophy of law. I have mentioned several factors that may contribute to this alienation. Let me end by mentioning one more.

Many law students think of themselves as training to work in the legal professions, and therefore think that every subject they study in law school should correlate to a possible professional specialization. That is how to get to be a partner in a law firm (they think) by age 35. This leads some to study, say, company law or intellectual property law on the footing that they are training to be company lawyers or intellectual property lawyers. This is not a wise way to look at legal education, or a legal career. Good lawyers can get to grips with just about any area of law as and when they need to. They can build up specialisation and expertise as they go along. They often end up specialising in things that they never contemplated specialising in as students. Recruiters know this and by and large are simply looking for people who are good at law, and good at analytical thinking more generally. You want to be good at law? Study contract, tort, property, crime, and constitutional law, and study hard. You want to be good at thinking more generally? Try taking off your stabilizers and *thinking without authority*. Learning how to do philosophy—remember, it is an activity, not a product—will help you in any analytical career.

Besides, you are at university. Take the opportunity to question every question while you still have the chance.

FURTHER READING

Lyons, David, *Ethics and the Rule of Law* (Cambridge: Cambridge University Press, 1984).

MacLean, Anne, *The Elimination of Morality: Reflections on Utilitarianism and Bioethics* (London: Routledge, 1993).

Nagel, Tom, *What Does It All Mean? A Very Short Introduction to Philosophy* (Oxford: Oxford University Press, 1987).

West, Robyn, *Normative Jurisprudence: An Introduction* (Cambridge: Cambridge University Press, 2011).

Wolff, Robert. P., *In Defense of Anarchism*, 2nd edn (Berkeley: University of California Press, 1998).

---

[1] Adrian van Hooydonk (BMW Director of Design), interviewed in *Wallpaper* Magazine, September 2011.

[2] Sir Alex Douglas-Home, "Foreword", in *Prosperity with a Purpose: Conservative Party General Election Manifesto 1964*.

[3] Jennifer Hart, franchisee of Ben and Jerry's Ice Cream in Galveston, Texas, interviewed in *The Daily News* [of Galveston], March 28, 2012.

[4] Google Inc, "Our Philosophy" at
*http://www.google.co.uk/about/corporate/company/tenthings.html* [Accessed on May 3, 2012].

[5] *http://www.philosophyskincare.co.uk/about-philosophy/about-us,default,pg.html* [Accessed on May 3, 2012].

[6] A translation from German of thesis 11 in Marx's "Theses on Feuerbach" written in 1845 and published as an appendix to Friedrich Engels, *Ludwig Feuerbach und der Ausgang der klassischen deutschen Philosophie* (Stuttgart 1888).

[7] Or possibly the abridged version edited by David McLellan (Oxford: Oxford World's Classics, 2008).

[8] Why? That is a philosophical question about law. For attention to it, see Joseph Raz, *The Authority of Law* (Oxford: Oxford University Press, 1979), 115–121.

[9] This memorable expression is from Robert Cover, "Violence and the Word" (1986) *Yale Law Journal* 95, 1601.

[10] A complaint about his new colleagues from the diary of legal philosopher H.L.A. Hart, written shortly after moving from Oxford's Philosophy Sub-Faculty to its Law Faculty in. Reported in Nicola Lacey, *A Life of H.L.A. Hart: The Nightmare and the Noble Dream* (Oxford: Oxford University Press, 2006), 157.

[11] The sceptics were a bunch of ancient philosophers who doubted whether anything can be known (as opposed to believed).

[12] Hart, "Legal and Moral Obligation" in A.I. Melden (ed), *Essays in Moral Philosophy* (Seattle: University of Washington Press, 1958), 82 at 86.

[13] (Oxford: Oxford University Press, 1961).

[14] A.W.B. Simpson, *Reflections on The Concept of Law* (Oxford: Oxford University Press, 2011), 80.

[15] A.W.B. Simpson, *Reflections on The Concept of Law* (Oxford: Oxford University Press, 2011), 140.

---

# 3. EMPIRICAL APPROACHES

*Simon Halliday*

## WHAT DO WE MEAN BY "EMPIRICAL"?

What do we mean by "empirical" approaches to the study of law? In general terms in relation to research and knowledge, the notion of "the empirical" is often contrasted with "the theoretical". In this broad contrast, "the empirical" relates to knowledge gained from observation or experimentation, whereas "the theoretical" relates to postulated knowledge derived through conceptual and analytical reasoning. Although this contrast may be useful in very general terms, it is probably confusing in the context of this book. As you will discover in the course of your legal studies, empirical data about law is often obtained for the purposes of exploring theoretical questions about law. Contrasting the empirical with the theoretical may not, then, be all that helpful here. An example can illustrate this point. Imagine that we are interested in society's response to crime. One of the theoretical questions about crime which we may ask is how to treat those who have been found guilty of crime. More specifically, we might ask a theoretical question about how to use imprisonment as a response to crime—should we use it extensively or minimally? This is a normative question—a question of how imprisonment *should* be used by the state. But to answer it, we may wish to collect or examine some empirical data about the extent to which imprisonment deters would-be criminals, or about the extent to which experiences of imprisonment prevent released criminals from turning back to crime.

The above example illustrates the fact that empirical questions can serve theoretical purposes. It is better, then, to define empirical approaches to the study of law positively rather than negatively—"what *does* it involve?", rather than "what does it *not* involve?" Accordingly, we should think of empirical approaches as involving empirical enquiry. In other words, empirical scholarship uses the research methods of the social sciences to obtain data about law and the legal system. Sometimes, the enquiry is simply about the collection of the data—just to find out what is happening empirically and to be able to describe it. Usually, however, as I have suggested, empirical data is collected so that it can be used to answer theoretical questions about law.

## THE RISE OF EMPIRICAL SCHOLARSHIP

Now that I have set out what we mean by "empirical" approaches to the study of law, I should say something about why they have become common within legal scholarship. Empirical scholarship about law has increased significantly over the last 50 years to the point where most law students will encounter some kind of empirical work during the course of their studies. The rise of empirical approaches within legal scholarship is largely the result of two parallel academic movements in the United Kingdom and the United States. These movements have been influential on each other in terms of ideas and research agendas. They have also been influential on the development of legal scholarship in the United Kingdom. I will look first at the rise of empirical scholarship on law in the United States because it is the older of the two movements.

The American law and society movement began in the 1960s and developed out of a group of sociologists who were interested in law. The vision of this small group, which was responsible for the creation of the *Law & Society Association*, was that the association would be multi-disciplinary in character. Law and society scholarship in the United States, more commonly known in the United Kingdom as "socio-legal studies", was really a movement of the general social sciences which recognised that many social scientific disciplines could have something to say about the operations and functions of law in society. Law school collaborators were quickly brought on board and encouraged to take part in the socio-legal enterprise. However, it is important to recognise that the law and society movement in the United States has drawn widely across the social sciences and is best considered as a particular feature of the social scientific study of society more generally.

The position in the United Kingdom was quite different. The development of socio-legal studies was evidenced mostly within the law schools. Socio-legal studies in the United Kingdom—and empirical work as an aspect of them—dates back to the early 1970s. In comparison to the United States, outwith a few notable exceptions,[1] the social sciences in the United Kingdom have not shown significant interest in law. It has been left to legal scholars in the main to pursue empirical enquiries about law. One of the reasons that empirical legal research has become so popular in UK law schools is that it offered a fresh and compelling approach to the study of law for some scholars. Indeed, it is probably helpful to think about the UK socio-legal movement as a reaction against the limits of pure doctrinal enquiry which had dominated legal scholarship previously. One, now prominent, socio-legal scholar describes what he sought from socio-legal work in the following terms:

> "a set of new perspectives on law to allow a breakout from the claustrophobic world of legal scholarship and education, as previously encountered. Most legal study … at the end of the 1960s seemed to focus on technicality as an end in itself and was unconcerned with fundamental questions about law's nature, sources, and consequences as a social phenomenon or about its moral groundings."[2]

In other words, the limits of technical legal enquiry failed to match the wider questions about law which had brought many students to law school in the first place. Increasingly, then, legal scholars began to recognise that the study of law raised a host of empirical questions which could not be answered by doctrinal scholarship. Indeed, a number of empirical assumptions about law were implicit to some doctrinal scholarship and some legal scholars set out to test these in a social scientific way. In 1990, given the wide interest in new approaches to legal scholarship, including empirical approaches, a *Socio-Legal Studies Association* was formed. This is now quite a large academic society in the United Kingdom which holds a conference every year and provides a forum for the development and dissemination of socio-legal research.

## EMPIRICAL RESEARCH AGENDAS

What kinds of questions about law have animated empirical scholarship over the years? This is a difficult question to answer in a short introductory chapter like this because empirical work has been very eclectic in character, both in terms of the research methods employed and the research questions asked. This should not be too surprising because the potential research agendas about law are, of course, limitless. As law and society change and as knowledge develops, new questions and concerns come to light. Nonetheless, at a very general level we can suggest some of the main themes which have driven empirical work about law. There are four suggested here.

### Creation of law

The first main theme is a curiosity about how law is created. At one level, the question of how law is created can be answered in a reasonably straightforward way. Indeed, the issue of what are the sources of law in a legal system is one of the first things which new students of law will learn. In the United Kingdom, students will learn a little, for example, about the creation of legislation in Parliamentary processes at Westminster and also at the devolved levels in relation to Scotland, Wales and Northern Ireland. They will further learn about law-making processes in the European Union. The notion of judge-made law will also be explored. These are all important matters. However, their treatment—particularly in relation to the creation of legislation—is often procedural in focus and comprises a description of the stages through which a proposal must go in order to become law.

Empirical research about the creation of law is generally quite different. It tends to look inside the decision-making processes which constitute the overall law-creation enterprise. Recognising that law-making is usually a complex *social* process where various individuals and groups have an input into the decision-making and where external groups try to influence these decisions, empirical researchers have tried to gain insights into how particular decisions are made, how proposals develop in particular ways, and what influences have made a difference to key decision-makers. At one level, empirical research has sought to expose the ways that law embodies the conflicts and differences of power and status in society. Challenging the image of law as somehow "natural" or as the embodiment of the rational expressions of legislative wisdom, empirical work has often revealed the ways in which emergent laws have been subject to contestation before legislatures or other bodies. Empirical scholars have focused on social and political forces in law-making. They have been interested, for example, in the mobilization of social movements and interest groups in order to influence the future content of legislation. The starting point of such research is the idea that law-making institutions set agendas and make decisions which are influenced by the structure of interest group participation. In other words, wider social forces shape the options and choices of decision-makers, resulting in law that bears the marks of those struggles. Empirical research can examine law-making activities in order to reveal these influences. Indeed, there is an element of overlap here between empirical work in this vein and the critical approaches to law which are described in the following chapter. Some of the empirical research on law making has been influenced by critical perspectives that look for a privileged position of certain groups in the social reality of law-making.

Empirical research about law creation might also examine the significance of the relationships between different constitutional bodies and the extent to which such relationships have influenced law making. For example, research about legislative process in the USA and the EU has focused on what is sometimes called the "judicialisation" of politics, whereby legislators have to operate within the context of the courts' powers to review legislative content. To what extent and in what ways does the prospect of judicial review influence the decisions of legislators about the content of legislation?

A final strand of empirical research on law-making—one which connects with some philosophical discussions about law—focuses on judge-made law. Much philosophical research about the nature of law has tried to unpack the legal reasoning processes which infuse judicial decision-making. Some empirical researchers have recognised that there is a strong empirical element to this enterprise and have conducted research which has tried to get inside the heads of judges. Such research empirically examines how judges make decisions and explores the significance to their ultimate judgments of matters such as legal arguments in courts or discussions about cases with their judicial peers.

**Implementation of law**
The second broad research theme relates to the implementation of law. A large and very varied group of officials are involved in the implementation of law. Perhaps most obviously, judges are involved. However, in empirical terms, judges may actually be the least significant officials engaged in legal implementation. Judges, though clearly very important within the legal system, see only a tiny fraction of cases. Most situations which could evolve into a legal dispute do not do so. Even within those that do, most

never reach the stage of litigation. Within those that make it to the litigation stage, most never make it to court. Judges sit at the top of a legal pyramid, if you like. But the routine business of legal implementation takes place at the bottom of the pyramid and usually remains unseen. In many situations, the "law" for ordinary citizens is what they experience in these routine everyday implementation decisions—decisions that are made by a host of people, from police officers, to social workers, to welfare benefits officers, to immigration officers, to planning officers, to health and safety inspectors, and so forth. Indeed, not all of the people involved in the implementation of law are public officials. Consider for a moment the question of employment rights. Employment law in the United Kingdom regulates the relationships between employers and employees, giving employees certain rights and entitlements and proscribing certain conduct on the part of employers. This law is generally implemented in the first instance by the human resources or personnel officers of the employer. Or, consider immigration law: although the government may place limits on who might enter the United Kingdom, some of the work of implementing these rules falls to airline personnel.

Our legal system, as we can begin to see, is a very complex business and extends well beyond the obvious examples of legal officials such as judges and the police. Indeed, we might suggest that the implementation of law— the lifeblood of our legal system—is so extensive and reaches so far into our routine, ordinary lives that, in many situations, it is almost invisible. However, many empirical researchers have seen the value of studying the various forms of legal implementation—what is sometimes called the "law in action". The goal is to study law at "street-level",[3] if you like, and to assess its significance for society from this perspective. This research agenda draws on the notion that these law jobs are, after all, just jobs. A realistic view of how these jobs are carried out would reveal that the various personnel charged with implementation are influenced by many things in addition to, or instead of, legal rules and principles. So, scholarship in this agenda seeks to unravel the social, political, economic and moral influences upon implementation. By doing so, it shows us that law, rather than being some kind of neutral force, standing over and above economic, social and moral relations in society, is actually inextricably bound up with them. Law cannot be put into action, cannot be brought to life, without these other features of society having a role to play. In other words, in the same way that we cannot properly understand society without examining the role of law in it, we cannot properly understand law without examining the role of society in it.

### Use of law

The third broad research agenda concerns the use of law. Empirical scholars have focused on ordinary citizens and their engagement with legal processes. We noted above that only a tiny fraction of potential legal disputes end up in court. This finding raises a number of important questions: why, when someone has a problem which is amenable to legal treatment, do they not turn to law for its resolution? Indeed, given that the majority of people seem *not* to use law to resolve their problems, perhaps the more pertinent question is about why people *do* in fact turn to law. The analysis of disputing behaviour and dispute resolution has been a mainstay of empirical scholarship about law for many years. Much of this research has debunked the notion of individuals as purely rational actors who will respond to their grievances in predictable ways. Equally, data about dispute resolution—about why, when and how legal processes are used—tell us much about the significance of law for society. They might, for example, cause us to reflect on the value and function of various legal opportunities for dispute resolution. Particularly in relation to situations where citizens might have grievances against public bodies, a connection can be made between empirical work and critical work on law. If, for example, rights of appeal against government decisions are used by only a tiny minority of citizens with grievances, then we might legitimately question who, in the round, benefits most from the appeal processes: is it the citizens who are subject to government decisions, or the public bodies themselves who, while offering a level of *procedural* propriety through rights of appeal, may continue with *substantively* problematic policies with relatively little challenge in the grand scheme of things? In other words, rights of appeal and other dispute resolution forums may be more symbolically important for certain groups and bodies than they are practically useful for the people who, theoretically, can use them.

**Social effects of law**
The final broad research theme concerns the social effects of law—the effects of law and legal processes on social life. At one level, this might involve an exploration of the extent to which particular legal measures have been effective in achieving the set of objectives which have been ascribed to them. If, for example, a particular legal provision has been created with a view to reducing a specific form of discrimination, or relieving the plight of a particular group in society, or changing the way that certain groups behave, then we might legitimately enquire about the extent to which we can observe those predicted results on the ground. Much of the empirical work in this vein has strong policy relevance. Policy-makers who craft laws to bring about social change have an interest in learning about the effectiveness of their policy innovations and so sometimes commission empirical researchers to conduct such enquiries. Equally, legal scholars may recognise that an issue of effectiveness has not been empirically researched and so may do so in order to inform policy makers.

Other research on the social effects of law is less clearly policy-driven, as such, but nevertheless might try to trace the impact of law on various aspects of social life. There is now quite a large body of work, for example, which questions the ability of the courts to bring about social change. The courts are often regarded—particularly by lawyers—as very powerful bodies which can bring about change through their decision-making. Public interest groups or social movement activists may pursue various forms of legal challenge in the courts in order to realise their particular political objectives. But, of course, the question of the extent to which success in court amounts to more than a pyrrhic victory is an empirical one. Empirical scholars must investigate the continuing plight, for example, of a group within society for whom a legal victory has been won before that question can be answered. Equally, in constitutional terms, many of us put our faith in the courts to uphold and protect the rule of law. For many in society, it is a source of comfort and encouragement that the courts can be turned to when the government acts unlawfully. This raises an empirical question, however, of how much influence the courts do, in fact, have over the working of government and other public bodies. To put it another way, to what extent can the courts control government behaviour? This particular set of questions has been the subject of research by a number of UK empirical legal scholars for many years now.

The above research has quite a tight focus and a clear "effectiveness" agenda. It generally starts with a particular set of legal provisions, or a particular type of legal action, or a particular court case and then proceeds to assess effectiveness towards a particular end. There are other ways, however, in which empirical scholars can explore the social effects of law. One might, for example, examine the ways in which certain aspects of law affect the way that people feel, behave or relate to each other. Research questions might include: how does the risk of legal liability and of having to pay out compensation affect the way that employers, or governments, or other organizations operate? How do various legal interventions through the welfare state affect people's sense of family and the importance of family? To what extent does the quality of legal procedures, in addition to the outcomes of these procedures, make a difference to people's sense of dignity and their faith in law?

Another rich vein of research over the last 25 years or so has been to examine how everyday ideas about law and legality shape ordinary people's sense of identity and how they relate to each other and public bodies. Regardless of what might happen in a court room, or a lawyer's office, or the police station, what do the commonplace characterisations of law that we find in society tell us about the ways in which legality shapes, constrains, enables or inspires social life? Indeed, we first need to ask what the basic characterisations of law in society are. Most scholars think that there are more than one—that there are different "stories" about law, if you like, which inform the ways we think about ourselves and our relations with each other. For example, in some situations we might think that the law is an objective and neutral force that stands for justice. In others, we might see it as a powerful but oppressive force which acts against us and which is to be resisted. Or, we might see it as something that can be played to our own advantage if we are clever enough. Equally, we might regard law as being unpredictable and arbitrary and as something to which we must simply surrender ourselves, hoping for the best. Regardless of whether we think these basic notions about legality are correct or exhaustive, the point here is that people's ideas about law and legality affect how they feel and behave. They help shape society in their own way. This is an important sense of the "social effects" of law and one that has inspired a great deal of interesting empirical work.

EMPIRICAL RESEARCH METHODS

I should not conclude this chapter without saying something very basic about the research methods of the social sciences which are used by empirical scholars to enquire about law. Unfortunately, the issue of social science research methods is a large and complex one—one to which entire textbooks are devoted. There is clearly, then, an important limit to what can be achieved in a short section of a short introductory chapter on empirical approaches to the study of law. So, let me be clear about what I aim to accomplish here. My goals are very modest: they are, first, to make the point that different research techniques exist; second, to note that different research techniques sometimes reflect different views about how we can understand the social world; and, third, to give you a flavour of the different research techniques which are used. This will not be enough to equip you to conduct social scientific research yourselves. Nor will it even equip you to adequately understand the debates surrounding social science research methods. However, it will, I hope, give you a very basic foundation from which you can build up your knowledge of research methods. This is an important thing to do—even for students of law. Even if you never conduct such research yourself, you need to be able to assess research evidence when you come across it in your studies. Knowing something about the different approaches taken to understanding the social world, including law, will help you do that.

The research techniques of the social sciences are often divided into two approaches: qualitative and quantitative. Quantitative research tries to understand society on the basis of a statistical analysis of a dataset. At its most basic level, it attempts to detect patterns of behaviour on the basis of statistical analysis. In other words, it can describe what is happening in society by collecting specific data—usually through surveys - and analysing them. For example, earlier in this chapter we noted the fact that most people who encounter problems which are amenable to legal resolution do not, in fact, turn to law to solve the problem. This is a quantitative claim. Researchers have collected data from a "sample" of society and analysed them. The data in question relate, first, to how often people encounter problems which are amenable to legal resolution and, second, to what they do about it. A "sample" is simply a selection of people which is deemed to share specific characteristics with the larger group of people which is being studied. This could be, as in this example, society as a whole, or it could be all women, or all lawyers, or all court users in a particular court, and so forth. The important point is that the "sample" is used as a proxy for the larger group. It is taken to represent the larger group and so, by analysing the sample, we can make a descriptive claim about the larger group—in this example, that most people do not turn to law despite having a legally resolvable problem.

At a more ambitious level, quantitative research goes beyond mere description and seeks to *explain* human behaviour on the basis of tracing statistically significant relationships between various factors in the dataset—"independent and dependent variables". The "dependent variable" is the particular feature of society which the researcher is trying to understand and explain. The "independent variables" are other features of society which may help explain the dependent variable. Let me return to the above example to make this point clearer. The dependent variable in the example is whether or not someone turns to law when they have a problem. The independent variables could include many things: the gender, ethnicity, educational background, employment status or income level of an individual or, indeed, the nature of the problem which the individual experiences. The goal of the researcher is to see if there are any statistically significant relationships between the dependent and independent variables. For example, are people more likely to turn to law if they have been educated to a high level, or if they earn a lot of money, or are white? Or, do the people who have turned to law share some combination of these factors?

Qualitative research techniques, by way of contrast, place a much greater emphasis on trying to *directly* access and report individuals' or groups' understanding of the world. Qualitative work is sometimes premised on the conviction that people's interpretations of the world can be quite varied—that social reality lies in variable perceptions rather than brute positive facts. For this reason, one cannot easily observe social reality from the outside, or understand it adequately by way of statistical analyses alone. Rather, qualitative research techniques try to somehow get inside the heads of their research subjects, to understand those people's particular interpretations of things, the motivations for their behaviour, and so forth. So whereas in quantitative research the engine of the explanatory work is the statistical analysis, in qualitative research the explanatory work is done by the research subjects themselves and the job of the researcher is to obtain as faithful an account of that as they can. There are a wide range of qualitative techniques which are used to this end. Indeed, new research techniques are being developed all the time. However, at a basic level, we can point to three main kinds of technique: interviews, observation and documentary analysis.

The basic notion of interviewing is pretty straightforward but different forms of interview exist. They can be semi-structured, unstructured or can involve groups. In semi-structured interviews, there will be a number of key questions or topics to be explored with a range of interviewees. However, there is also considerable room within that structure for the data to be particular to individual interviewees. Some degree of comparability between interviewees is retained through the structure of the interview schedule or "topic guide", as it is sometimes called, but interviewees are more active participants in revealing the complexities of their own perceptions of things in response to questions and probing. Unstructured interviews, by way of contrast, are entirely open-ended in character. Interviewees respond to initial questions in their own terms and discuss issues according to their own frames of reference. In this sense, interviewees have much greater control over the interview process. Group interviews are, as the name suggests, interviews with groups of people rather than with individuals. Although they are sometimes conducted for pragmatic reasons to do with time and money, they can also be useful for obtaining data on group interactions and ideas that are promulgated and developed in a group setting. The data which one might gain from an individual in an interview may be quite different from what one would obtain from the same individual in a group setting.

Observation involves learning about people, their ideas and behaviour by watching them. Unlike quantitative researchers, observational researchers tend not to begin their projects with hypotheses to be tested. Instead, they approach their subjects with an open mind about what is important. The development of ideas about what is happening in a social setting, about the meanings of certain practices and symbols, is generally a slow and incremental process. The analysis is grounded in and dictated by the language and behaviour the research subjects. Most observational researchers would think that observations give more reliable data than interviews, in that interviews only offer a person's account of something after the event. This is not necessarily the same as the practice being described in interview. It may be a sanitised version of events. Interviewees may recall practices as they would like them to be, rather than as they actually are. Equally, there is a limit to how well the complexities and inconsistencies of social practices can be captured in interviews. The benefit of observational work, by way of contrast, is that one accesses life in all its complexities as it actually happens.

Documentary analysis, in its widest sense, simply entails the analysis of texts as part of the research process. Documents, then, can be almost anything. However, commonly within socio-legal research, researchers might examine policy documents of public agencies or business organisations, publicity documents, media stories, and so forth. We can probably make a useful distinction between two basic approaches to the significance of texts. The first treats texts as the representation of objective reality. Documents, in this sense, are one way of us learning objective facts about the social world. An example of this would be, for example, where a researcher uses a policy document of a business or public agency as describing the values and practices of the organisation in question. In this approach, the focus of the research is the facts of the social world, and the document is one way of discovering this objective truth that is "out there", so to speak. In other approaches, however, the document itself is the focus of enquiry because it represents only one set of perceptions—or one reality, if you like—amongst others. One way of thinking about this is not to ask, "what does this document tell us about the objective world?", but rather to ask, "what interpretive work is this document doing in this particular social context?", or "how is reality being socially constructed in this document?"

The above is no more than a sketch of the empirical research methods employed by researchers to further our knowledge of law and society. Further work will be required on your part to consolidate your grasp of some of the debates surrounding research methods. This will permit you to read and assess empirical data with greater confidence and ability, which, in turn, will deepen your knowledge of law in society.

## CONCLUSION

In the previous chapter, John Gardner made reference to Karl Marx's exhortation to move beyond philosophy's preoccupation with merely understanding the world so as to actually transform it. Whereas philosophers are more concerned with understanding, critical legal scholars, as you will discover in the next chapter by Donald Nicolson, are more concerned with transformation. Empirical scholarship about law lies somewhere in between the two, or, perhaps more accurately, straddles the two. Some empirical scholars are of the view that a proper understanding of society (of which law is a very significant element) is a difficult enough task in itself. Others, influenced by critical theory, seek an understanding of law in society because of a more fundamental drive to expose and ameliorate social unfairness and injustice (to which law is, they claim, a significant contributor). The core conviction, however, which underpins all empirical research on law is the need, first and foremost, to understand it in its social context. Law is created, implemented, and used by people and groups of people, while all of us feel its effects. Law is, in short, profoundly social. This is why the social sciences and empirical research are an essential part of our toolkit for studying law. Even if you never conduct empirical research yourself (and most law students don't) there are a sufficient number of academics who do that you will come across a lot of such work in your law degrees. This chapter should give you a head start in engaging with it.

## FURTHER READING

Abel, R.L. (ed), *The Law and Society Reader* (New York: NYU Press, 1995).
Calavita, K., *Invitation to Law and Society: An Introduction to the Study of Real Law* (Chicago: University of Chicago Press, 2010).
Cane, P. and Kritzer, H. (eds), *Oxford Handbook of Empirical Legal Research* (Oxford: Oxford University Press, 2010).
Galligan, D., "Introduction" (1993) *Journal of Law and Society* (Special Issue), Vol.22, No.1, pp.1–16.
Serron, C., *The Law and Society Canon* (Aldershot: Ashgate, 2006).

---

[1]  Social scientists in the United Kingdom have maintained their interest in crime and deviancy. Equally, social scientists along with lawyers have developed the empirical study of regulation. They have also been prominent in the study of the implementation of social policy legislation and in issues concerned with family law.

[2]  Cotterrell, R., "Subverting Orthodoxy, Making Law Central: A View of Sociolegal Studies" (2002) *Journal of Law & Society*, Vol.29, No.4, 632–44 at 633.

[3]  This refers to an important book about public administration called *Street-Level Bureaucracy* by Michael Lipsky (New York: Russell Sage Foundation, 1980).

# 4. CRITICAL APPROACHES

*Donald Nicolson*

## INTRODUCTION

The notion of "critical" approaches to the study of law does not have an absolutely clear, agreed upon meaning. Nonetheless, we use it in this chapter—as do many other scholars—to refer to assorted theories which are critical of various aspects of Western society and law's role in giving effect to and legitimising certain forms of power and injustice. It usually denotes those who are critical of law and society from a more or less left wing perspective. Critical approaches to law—or critical legal theory, as it is often termed—have been hugely influential in legal scholarship. Even if writers do not identify themselves as critical scholars, the approaches they use in exposing contradiction or exploitation are now a very common way of approaching law.

Before examining some of these approaches in greater detail, it will useful to have an idea of the target of much of critical legal theory. The target is the core of the orthodox approach to law. This has been termed "liberal legalism" or "legal liberalism" and can be said to involve two basic ideas. The first, "legalism", more commonly called "formalism", sees law as consisting solely of authoritative legal texts such as cases and statutes. These are seen as capable of being understood and applied in a value-free manner to the facts of cases solely through the application of logic. Formalism treats law as capable of being studied and understood in terms of its own rules. Critique within formalism is limited to ensuring that law is logically applied and that legal rules coherently hang together. Theory within formalism is limited to providing definitions of various concepts in law such as property, intention, etc.—what is known as analytical jurisprudence. All critical legal theories reject this idea that the law regulates society in a neutral, value-free way. Instead, they see such law as reflecting the values of those making law, and these values in turn as reflecting dominant social values. Nor do they accept that law can be understood as separate from the society in which it exists. In this way, there are some clear links between critical approaches to law and some of the ideas underpinning empirical research about law, discussed in the previous chapter.

The rejection of formalism, it should be noted, is by no means confined to critical legal theories alone. It is, in fact, shared by many contemporary legal theorists. However, critical legal theorists differ from other legal theorists as regards the second aspect of orthodox legal theory, namely "liberalism". Liberalism holds that the aim of law and other social arrangements is to maximise human freedom. Given that each person has his/her own values and interests, it is thought wrong for law to interfere and impose a particular set of values on society. Instead, under liberalism the only justification for law's interference is to prevent harm and to protect each person from being harmed by others and the state. Also central to liberalism is the idea that everyone is equal under the law and that no one should be treated more favourably because of their background or other factor. It is these ideas which form the main focus of the arguments of critical legal theory.

In the remainder of this chapter we will examine four major critical approaches and their treatment of law: Marxism, feminism, critical legal studies, and postmodernism. Our aim is to illustrate how a critical approach to law can help us understand how law operates and enable us to make more widely informed judgements about the value of law in general and specific law and procedures in particular.

## MARXISM

Marxism was the first critical theory to emerge. Marxism is primarily a theory of history which argues that the core to understanding history and society is economics. And the core to understanding the economy, in turn, is to examine how society organises the production of its means of survival—food, clothing, shelter, etc. Production in capitalist societies involves some people owning what Marx called the "means of production"—such as land and tools—and others working for them for a wage. The owners Marx called the "bourgeoisie" or "capitalists" and the workers he called the "proletariat" or "working class". By paying workers less for their labour than the money gained by selling the product of their labour, the capitalist is able to make a profit and thus live off the sweat of the worker. In this way, Marx characterised capitalist societies as being sustained by oppression and the suppression of the working class.

While Marx's ideas on law, specifically, were rudimentary and inconsistent, later writers sought to develop a Marxist critique of law. These Marxist analyses of law have changed and developed over the years and, at times, have been rather complex. Indeed, it is not possible in a short chapter such as this to do justice to this rich vein of critical thinking. Instead, we will focus on one approach to law, inspired by Marx, which has endured in critical legal theory and which remains influential. It is to concentrate on law's role as *ideology*. By "ideology" we mean, very broadly, the ideas by which we make sense of the world. According to Marxists, while ideology might involve philosophies like liberalism or other well thought out views, it also contains much less conscious values, opinions, attitudes, assumptions and prejudices. According to Marxists, those in power seek to influence ideology to ensure that their view of the world is accepted by all in society so that most people see the status quo as somehow normal. Rather than trying to rule solely through repression, which is often ineffective, the ruling class will seek to use various institutions such as the law, the family, schools, churches, and the media to influence the attitudes, ideas and values of the subordinate classes. However, the subordinate classes are not always easily fooled. To be successful, the ruling class must present its own interests as being to the benefit of all. For this to work it must incorporate some of the interests of the subordinate classes, thus sacrificing some of its own interests. This is why the ruling class, when it can afford to do so, accepts the welfare state and other laws which seem to go against its direct interests.

The second way in which law acts as ideology is through adopting a universalistic form. Laws treat all people as equal to each other, and most legal rules apply to all regardless of class, race, sex, etc. Thus despite its role in sustaining capitalist relations of production and favouring the interests of capitalists, law presents itself as embodying the interests of all in the community. Law protects the person and property of all. It treats equally the employer's capital and the worker's personal belongings. This creates the impression that all have a common interest in the protection of private property. Similarly, when law protects the interests of the ruling class, it presents them as the interests of all. The regulation of trade union power under the banner of individual freedom for workers, such as through rules on strike balloting, is seen as legitimate since everyone values freedom. In ways such as this, law's universal form acts to de-politicise its content and application. Law's universal form is given specific emphasis by the important notion of the Rule of Law, which portrays law as being applied to all equally without fear and favour. Concomitant with this view is the notion of the courts as the protector of the individual against the state. However, Marxists argue that even if the Rule of Law were always upheld—which it is not—and people were governed in terms of law rather than arbitrary discretion, this would only provide for formal or procedural justice. It does not detract from the fact that the laws themselves might be substantively unjust. In fact, by focusing attention on the formal justice contained in the Rule of Law notion, attention is focused away from the existence of substantive legal injustice. Again, we can see links here with some empirical work on law discussed in the previous chapter.

A third way in which law acts as ideology is through the formalistic idea that law comprises a rational set of principles. As such, it is presented as being certain and thus ensuring the necessary predictability to allow people to plan their economic and other activities. Again, the focus is on the logic of the rules rather than their content. This rationality is also important in terms of the role of the courts because if law is rational, it can be portrayed as capable of being applied logically and hence neutrally by judges. It is thus irrelevant that judges have tended to come from the ranks of the capitalist class or the middle classes whose interests are aligned with them. In reality, say Marxists, law is as political as a speech by a politician. However, law has its own language, techniques and procedures that are very different to everyday politics. One cannot simply read legislation or precedents like a political speech—one has to be inducted into the mysteries of legal method. Law is thus impenetrable to the layperson. Because of this, legal solutions can be presented solely as technical issues, understandable only to its technicians, thus obscuring the political nature of the solutions. Thus in criminal law, for example, the query as to why starvation is no defence to theft can be explained, not in terms of the defence of private property, but as involving the technical and, by implication, neutral distinction between motive and intention.

Looking at these ideas forces us to rethink some of the cherished values of law. Most importantly, it encourages us to look behind the surface appearance of legal claims to see how they actually pan out in reality. This is an important methodological tool. Marxists argue that law tends to reflect society, not as it actually exists, but only as it appears, thus obscuring its essential oppressive features.

## FEMINISM

Many of these criticisms are also adopted by feminists. Like Marxists, they are motivated to expose and end oppression and injustice, though obviously they are concerned about women rather than the working class. Equally, at least since the 1970s, feminists have argued that that law is part of the problem and not just the solution to sexism. Much feminist work on law has focused on uncovering the "maleness" of law itself and on suggesting ways to ensure that law is reformed in the light of moral principles which allegedly reflect female ways of thinking. Feminists adopted a variety of approaches to these questions. However, one which provides a useful contrast to many accepted orthodox legal approaches is that of psychological or cultural feminism. This approach is associated primarily with the psychologist Carol Gilligan. She argued that, whether through nature or nurture, women have developed a different way of thinking and a different set of moral values and that these are excluded from, or at least subordinated, by the law. Thus she attacked the idea so well entrenched in Western philosophy that women have a less developed sense of justice and morality in that they are unable to distance themselves from their emotions in order to make proper moral judgements. Moral philosophers and moral psychologists had previously argued that the highest form of moral development involves making rational, objective, unemotional and impersonal judgements about rights and abstract principles. Gilligan called this mode of moral thinking the *ethic of justice* and criticised it as being masculine. She pointed out that moral psychologists developed this idea about moral development by only studying boys. On the basis of a number of experiments with both boys and girls, however, Gilligan asserted that there is another way of moral thinking which is marked by concern for the concrete needs of those with whom one comes into contact, rather than respect for their abstract rights. What she called the *ethic of care* is based on connectedness, subjective emotion and responsibility for maintaining relationships.

The major difference between the ethic of justice and the ethic of care is that, whereas the former is founded on the idea that everyone should be treated the same, the latter requires that no one should be hurt. This means that, in moral dilemmas, whereas men tend to stand on principle irrespective of the consequences, women are more pragmatic in being most concerned to protect their loved ones from harm and to ensure that if anyone is going to be harmed it should be the one who can best bear the harm. In short, Gilligan argued that women speak in a different moral voice and that feminists needed to ensure that this voice was heard. Gilligan did not argue that the ethic of care should replace the ethic of justice, only that the ethic of care should be placed *alongside* the ethic of justice.

Gilligan's work has been incorporated into the ideas of many other theorists. Her ideas also provide a basis for a powerful critique of the law as reflecting male ways of thinking. For example, it can be argued that imprisonment of offenders justified by reference to an abstract notion of "just desserts" is actually unjust when applied to women because women feel the separation from their loved ones much more than men. It also has provided a platform to reform the law. Thus it has been argued that the adversarial system of justice, in which the winner takes all following an aggressive assertion of rights by two protagonists, is very much a male way of doing things. It subordinates a full investigation of the situation and the needs of the parties to a competitive battle over who is to win in terms of abstract legal principles. Women, it is argued, tend to be more interested in concrete situations than abstract principles and therefore in finding all relevant facts and the best possible solution for all those involved. Thus the ethic of care would encourage negotiation or mediation as way of solving legal problems rather than adversarial litigation.

Nonetheless, some feminists have criticised the association of the ethic of care with women. Indeed, another important feminist theorist, Catherine MacKinnon, argued that when women speak with a different voice it is, in fact, the voice given to them by men. It is a voice that has been trained by men for male interests. According to MacKinnon, men have constructed women as different from them and then have used these very differences to justify their domination of women. Thus, there is an obvious link between the ethic of care and the attributes required in the family and home, which happen to be the area of society where people are unpaid or underpaid and lack much social power. Mackinnon called her brand of feminism "radical feminism". Her argument was not, however, the crude one of men using law as a blunt instrument to further their own interests. The maleness of law, according to MacKinnon, went further than the content of its rules and extended to its methodology. In particular, law presents itself as dispassionate, disinterested, impersonal and objective while, in reality, it is gender-biased. This is problematic for women in two ways. First, the claim to objectivity is dangerous because it obscures reality. Secondly, even if law were to achieve objectivity, neutrality and a dispassionate perspective, MacKinnon argued that this is not necessarily a good thing. Men might think that the best way to solve problems is by being distanced from them. Women, on the other hand, recognise the need to participate and become involved in problems—that it is better to identify with a problem than to treat it as something to be dealt with coolly and abstractly. MacKinnon thus wanted law to reflect female ways of thinking. Implicit in this argument is a view that a female perspective on law is better than the male perspective

- that the qualities that women possess would provide the basis for a more desirable legal system. For this reason, like Gilligan, Mackinnon ran into the criticism that she "essentialises" both women and men—in other words, she sees both as having some natural essence. The difficulty with such a position is not only that it ignores the fact that not all men see women in the way that Mackinnon argues, but it also assumes that all women have similar experiences, desires and needs. The counter argument is that there are as many factors *dividing* women as uniting them. For example, Muslim, Afro-Caribbean, Jewish, Irish, gay and working class women all have very difference experiences which cannot be collapsed into a single feminist view.

These flaws were particularly problematic for postmodern feminists. Postmodernism rejects the idea that anything has an essence. Instead it recognises the contradictory, arbitrary and complex nature of social phenomena. Postmodern feminists do not question the argument that law is ultimately sexist and operates as a powerful force in society to keep women in an inferior position. However they argue that this relationship is not a simple one of cause and effect. Rather, it is complex, contradictory and multifaceted. For instance, Carol Smart has shown that law has been used to *improve* the position of women in society such as by improving their rights to financial support and child custody on divorce. It has also been used to protect women against the worst excesses of male physical and sexual abuse. However, contained in these new legal reforms was a view of women as economic and social subordinates to men, with men as breadwinners in the marketplace and women confined to the role of mother and housewife. Thus, Smart argued, while law was in some respects positively reforming women's position in the family, it was, at the same time, being used to keep women in their place in the family. By looking at the history of legal reforms in these and other areas, postmodern feminists are led to a position which is ultimately wary of law. Thus, they argue, women should be very careful before turning to law for a solution—it frequently takes away as much as it gives.

An example of such wariness is postmodern feminism's position on rights. On the one hand, feminists recognise the advantages of women seeking to fight oppression through the claim for legal rights. Couching one's claim in terms of rights makes it readily understandable. The language of rights is a political language that everyone understands. Rights have an emotional appeal in that they seem to provide protection for the weak against the powerful. On the other hand, there are many problems with rights. Some of feminism's criticisms echo those of Marxists, namely that rights divide people—that they are held by individuals and hence can only benefit individual women, not women as a whole. Equally, legal rights do not solve problems. They merely turn social problems into ones defined as having a legal solution. And whatever the law provides may not in fact do much to solve the original problem. For example, giving a woman a right to obtain an interdict or injunction against her violent partner does not stop the violence in the first place, while to imprison him if be breaches the interdict or injunction will not prevent him returning later. In fact, rights can often make things worse by suggesting that a solution to the problem has been found, thus inhibiting further and more effective action. Here again we can see links with empirical work on law discussed in the previous chapter.

A second example of the wariness of postmodern feminism towards law relates to the ways in which law helps construct stereotypical and frequently harmful notions of masculinity and femininity. Gender constructions do not just affect how the law is applied. They also reinforce social conceptions of appropriate gender behaviour. The message contained in legal judgments and rules filters through to general public knowledge, via the media and various forms of popular culture such as novels and films—a theme which is explored further in the next chapter of this book. Given law's authoritative social status, law helps educate society as to the norms of appropriate femininity and masculinity.

## CRITICAL LEGAL STUDIES

By contrast to Marxism and Feminism which are largely "single-issue" theories, there are two critical approaches to law which draw on and influence writers and activists motivated by a wide variety of concerns. The first is critical legal studies. This should not be confused with critical legal theory more generally. Critical legal studies is only one strand within critical legal theory. Moreover, CLS (as it is usually called) is not a coherent and specific theoretical position. It is more of a political grouping of mainly US academics who met at conferences and wrote from a left wing perspective during the 1980s. It includes Marxists and what are known as "fem crits", "race crits". However, one idea which did unite them is worth exploring because of its implications for legal research methods. This is the idea that liberal society suffers from a fundamental contradiction. This stems from that fact that as CLS guru Duncan Kennedy puts it, "relations with others are both necessary to and incompatible with our freedom." Liberalism, as we have seen, espouses individual freedom. However, if everyone has maximum freedom, physically or otherwise, strong members of society are likely to use their freedom to limit that of the weak. Thus we need to ensure that freedom is not abused. And we do this through various forms of community control. In other words, individual freedom is dependent on the existence of a communal coercive order to enforce it. We also need institutions like the state to protect us and our freedom. But at the same time that these institutions protect our freedom, they also threaten our freedom. Laws designed to protect freedom simultaneously limit freedom. Moreover, they may do so far more than is necessary to ensure maximum freedom—either through abuse of power or simple miscalculation.

In other words, the relationship between freedom and the community is always one of contradiction: communities are necessary to freedom, but they also threaten freedom. Liberals present this contradiction as a cosy competition between individual and communal interests that can be rationally compromised or mediated. They paint a picture of Western law as a natural and hence neutral blend of rules, principles and rights which preserve individual autonomy and secure the general welfare. By contrast, CLS argues that liberal law can never resolve the contradictions within law: they remain in irresolvable tension and help explain why law is rarely clear and consistent. Building on Kennedy's idea, other writers have pointed to a whole host of other legal contradictions. Examples include the eternal debate between subjectivity and objectivity in all areas of law, the public/private divide in family and criminal law, the due process *versus* criminal control models in criminal law, etc. What this shows, according to CLS, is that all legal solutions are in fact political choices between competing values, though they also argue that the law tends to favour individual over community, yet seeks to hide this bias behind claims to legal and judicial neutrality.

## POSTMODERNISM

The second cross-cutting strand of critical legal theory is postmodern legal theory. Again, this does not have a particular interest, such as in race or class. Instead there are postmodernist feminists, postmodern race theorists, and even postmodern Marxists—sometimes called post-Marxists. Indeed, we have already seen the influence of postmodernism in feminist legal theory. However, we need to explore it separately here.

Postmodernism does not denote a particular set of political beliefs or even theoretical aims. Rather, what is distinctive about postmodernism is its approach to questions of knowledge, truth and reason, to politics and morality, and its development of the distinctive methodology called "deconstruction". Postmodernism, as its name suggests, marks a rejection of modernism. Modernism represented the belief in the power of humans to understand, explain and exploit the world. Thus in the 18th century the Enlightenment replaced the old beliefs in nature, God, etc. with a belief in humans. Humans were thought capable of understanding the world completely. The Enlightenment began an age of optimism, in which people began to believe that they controlled their own destiny and could make the world a wonderful place to live in. The way that humans were going to achieve this progress was through reason and science. Reason enabled man to discover objective truth and universally valid values which underlay human existence. From science, modernism took the idea that human knowledge can be gained in a neutral, value-free manner. Science was used as a model for all forms of knowledge and all disciplines. Science became an important guarantee of the status of a particular form of knowledge. Moreover it was believed that, not only was the world made up of objectively true facts, but also that there were also objectively true moral and political values.

Motivated by the 20th century failures and abuses of science and also the failure of political experiments purportedly based on the objective truth of socialism, people began to be sceptical about modernism and enlightenment values. This lead to what has come to be known as postmodernism. Very broadly it is marked by the following features: first, postmodernists distrust large-scale theories that have been constructed to explain and reform the world. Flowing from the failure of large-scale ideas like communism or capitalism to provide the way to progress, postmodernists are suspicious about any attempts to deal with ideas or problems on a large scale. These theories postmodernists call "grand narratives" to denote that they cannot purport to be anything like objective or neutral truth—they are simply someone's story about the world. Moreover, they present complex life in a coherent and structured way just as stories abstract from a variety of facts to provide a narrative with a beginning, middle and end.

Linked to this is a rejection of the clear divide between systems of thought like philosophy, on the one hand, and literature, on the other hand. Influenced by Nietzsche, postmodernists see philosophy as resembling literature in that it tells stories, not truth. Postmodernism prefers provisional small-scale theories that pay attention to people's experiences and to the diversity of human existence and experience. It focuses on the local rather than the global. It seeks to understand things by looking at them at a micro rather than a macro level. Knowledge must be based upon individual experience rather than on grand abstract ideas, which take no account of what is really happening in people's lives. Postmodernism sees social phenomena as too diverse, contradictory, complex and arbitrary to be brought together in some central theory of the world.

Moreover, postmodernists deny that there are such things as "facts" out there. Instead of facts, they suggest there are only interpretations. The world does not have one meaning, they argue, but myriad meanings. Consequently, postmodernists contend that in order to understand things one should not seek to find one overarching interpretation from one particular perspective—philosophical, sociological, religious, or legal, etc. Truth, they argue, is relative to society and its culture. Truth is *socially* constructed rather than existing in objectivity somewhere "out there" just waiting to be discovered. More specifically, language is not simply a means of communication involving a neutral conduit pipe through which ideas pass. Language inculcates ideas and values. For example, positions of authority and many public sphere occupations are often described by words like "chairman", "policeman", and "ombudsman". Similarly, law always uses the masculine pronoun and speaks of the "reasonable man". This helps inculcate the view that men are naturally more important than woman, that they occupy positions of authority and the more prestigious public sphere occupations, and that their behaviour is the social norm.

Importantly, this focus on language and the social construction of truth leads us to "deconstruction", the central methodology of postmodernism. Deconstruction involves a new way of reading texts and language which breaks with the assumptions that there is strict, albeit arbitrary, correlation between meaning and language, and that the aim of interpretation is to discover the author's intent. Deconstruction was developed by Jacques Derrida. Derrida rejects the idea that a text has one immutable meaning which is laid down by its author and that a text can be read or understood on its own. He says that all texts are written against the background of other earlier texts. Writers who create texts or who use words do so on the basis of all other texts and words they have encountered. Similarly, readers who interpret texts do so on the basis of their knowledge of other texts. Texts, once produced, set off to create their own life. This is because whenever we write or speak our words do not always convey what we want to get across. We may also convey additional meanings we do not or could not possibly intend. A famous aphorism of deconstructionism is that the birth of the reader is the death of the author. This can be seen in the legal practice of laying down precedents. When, for example, Lord Atkin laid down his neighbour principle in the famous case of *Donoughue v Stevenson*, not only were there many different versions of the reasoning contained in his judgment, but it was impossible to tell how the judgment would be interpreted. Lord Atkin could no longer control the development of the doctrine and it was left to later judges to decide what the law should be, all the while purporting to interpret his judgment.

Deconstruction seeks to provide a careful reading of texts to ascertain what other meanings or texts are contained in the interpreted text and what meanings are left out. This is based upon the idea that words do not have meaning in their own but derive their meaning from their opposite. For instance, "active" means nothing without a reference to "passive". As a result throughout Western philosophy there are numerous ideas that are set up against another idea in a relationship of difference—what are called "dualities" or "binary oppositions". Examples include: reason/passion; objective/subjective; man/woman. However, as the examples show, these binary oppositions are not set up in a relationship of equality, but a relation of domination and subordination. The aim of deconstruction is to challenge the implicit hierarchy in these dualities and hence to subvert the aim of the text containing one side of the duality. Because one term always depends on its opposite, there will always be a trace of the subordinate idea in the dominant. Once the subordinate idea is identified, the deconstructionist will seek to reverse the hierarchy in order to challenge the privileged idea. Derrida argues that the "deconstructive reversal" often shows that the reasons for privileging one idea turn out to apply equally to the subordinate idea. In other words, one can reverse the hierarchy and use the reasons currently given for the dominance of one side of the opposition to argue that it should be subordinate. Similarly, the alleged vices of the subordinate side can also be shown to be the vices of the privileged side. In this form of "immanent critique", arguments can be shown to undo themselves and one can challenge many of the hierarchies of Western philosophy and law.

Deconstruction has important political implications. The aim of deconstruction is to break the power of the author to impose meanings. This is important because it empowers the reader and allows for a greater possibility of popular participation in the creation of meaning. This helps to challenge the power of others to impose their ideas on us through the construction of meaning and through what postmodernists describe as the "construction of the subject". Postmodernists argue that people are as much created by language as language is constructed by people. For example, the way that boys and girls are talked about and treated helps turn them into highly gendered subjects. As we have already seen, law is a very powerful form of "subject construction". It tells us what we are and how we are to behave. According to postmodernist legal theorists, it is through texts and other legal discourses that the legal subject is defined, captured, circulated and judged. The aim of postmodern legal theory is thus to provide a critical reading and rewriting of the texts of law. This is achieved by challenging both the substantive content of law—its construction of the legal subject—and the categories, classification and methods of law.

Postmodernist legal theory is based on the belief that within the classical texts of law are excluded voices, submerged histories and ideas, which can be "re-discovered" and used to challenge orthodox ideas in law. Alongside orthodox and conscious ideas in law are always the unorthodox and the unconscious. Postmodernist legal theory aims to uncover these hidden ideas. It attends to the marginal, the peripheral or the surface in order to recapture the politics which has escaped the text or has been hidden beneath its ritual terminology.

The aim of such analyses is not totally negative or mindless critique. Postmodernist legal theory realises that in "re-reading" law, it is also rewriting law and, in doing so, it also communicates a body of knowledge on law. In other words, reading law itself involves a writing of law and that writing can put forward alternative visions of law. Consequently, postmodern writers cannot avoid the question of legal reform. They are always involved in reform and therefore need to attend to questions like how they want the legal subject to be reconstituted, what law should look like in a postmodern world and what ethics are applicable. Indeed, a primary aim of postmodern legal theory is an attempt to bring ethics and justice back into law. They argue that the very notion of law is predicated upon ethics and justice. Before we get law, we get issues of ethics and justice. Without such issues, there is no need for law. But what orthodox legal theory has done is to separate the issues of law, ethics and justice. It says that they are not connected. Yet at the same time it creates the impression that law *is* justice; that legal behaviour *is* ethical behaviour. And thus to act justly or ethically is simply to follow the law. This leaves no space for the individual to decide how to act according to his or her own sense of morality and justice. Postmodernist legal theory, therefore, calls for a return to a concern for ethics and justice.

FURTHER READING

Hunt, A., "Law, State and Class Struggle" (1976) *Marxism Today* 178.
Hunt, A., "The Theory of Critical Legal Studies" (1986) 6 *Oxford Journal of Legal Studies* 1.
Morrison, W., *Jurisprudence: From the Greeks to Postmodernism* (London: Cavendish, 1997), Ch.10 (on Marxism).
Smart, C., *Feminism and the Power of Law* (London: Routledge, 1989) Ch.4.
Ward, I., *An Introduction to Critical Legal Theory* (London: Cavendish, 2004), pp.137–144, Ch.7.

# 5. LAW AND POPULAR CULTURE

*Peter Robson*

## INTRODUCTION

It is a paradox that what might seem to be the newest approach to studying and understanding law has, in fact, been with us in some senses since the emergence of formal legal education in the 19th century. Its paradoxical nature continues when we consider its current impact on legal study and its likely future. The reasons for all this apparent confusion stems from the different ways in which the expression "law and popular culture" can be used. There is a traditional version of law and popular culture happily operating alongside a new "upstart" version. One deals with law and literature, while the other focuses on law and the visual media—film and television. We will examine both in this chapter.

So how do we clear up this mysterious paradox? Start at the beginning with the older version of law and popular culture and how it developed. University degrees in law have only been with us in the United Kingdom since the 1870s. Before then, a limited number of universities had faculties of law and professors who wrote on a range of practical and philosophical issues. What they did not have, however, were students. They did not offer degrees. There were some desultory courses offered to trainee lawyers but the reports to the Scotch Universities Commission in 1863 and the Universities Commission in 1873 from the great institutions of learning in the middle of the 19th century paint a sorry picture. When universities started to offer courses in law in the 1870s the degree was in the style we are familiar with today from the United States—the postgraduate first degree (that is, studying for a second undergraduate degree, already having obtained one in another subject). It was argued at the time that there was a need for would-be lawyers to reflect on the nature of law and its relationship with justice. However, the young men who took these degrees—and they were, by order of the courts, all men—had already received their education at university, usually in an arts subject, and so were in some sense already "educated". The law degree, then, concentrated on those areas of practice which were central to the working life of the lawyer without needing to worry about whether or not it inculcated an inquiring frame of mind in the student. The details of the operation of the legal system were focused on and the course was geared towards teaching professional practical subjects to the graduates who had commenced working in the legal profession. Teaching on these part-time degrees was typically undertaken at the beginning of the day and at teatime to enable these graduates to combine their study with full-time work as legal apprentices.

The alternative approach into the legal profession at the time was an in-house training route. Here would-be lawyers completed a period of service in legal firms as articled clerks or apprentices while taking examinations set by the local legal professional societies. Despite the development of the university route in the late 19th century, many opted for this in-house route. It was not until the late 1950s and 1960s that legal education as a distinct degree for school leavers was developed and became a more widespread route into the profession. This expansion of legal education through the universities offered a further opportunity to address the question of what should be taught to aspiring lawyers. The debates about what should be in the legal syllabus addressed the crucial issue of balance. On the one hand, there was a continuing need to focus on professional training to meet the day-to-day practical concerns of the legal profession which desired useful well-trained new recruits from university. On the other hand, it was recognised that there was also a need for would-be lawyers to reflect on the nature of law and its relationship with justice. The terms of these discussions were partly driven by what had happened with an unreflective approach to the nature of law and legality and the complicit legal profession in the Nazi era in Germany. The consensus was that there should be more to the new school leavers' law degree than merely providing training for the profession. A deeper and wider education was required and this was achieved through the inclusion of compulsory subjects like jurisprudence (the philosophy of law) and, somewhat bizarrely, forensic medicine. These would allow the formation of fully rounded lawyers for the future, capable of critical reflection and contemplation above the narrow details of the common law and emerging statutory codes and the dangerous view that "the law is the law".

## LAW AND LITERATURE

One of the by-products of the 19th century debates was the notion that popular culture could provide an insight into the legal process. As far back as 1913 John Marshall Gest's *The Lawyer in Literature* started a stream of writing about law which showed the link to literature. This early collection of the more literary thinking from within the legal community was very much in the spirit of establishing the lawyer as a fully rounded scholar. With its roots in Gest's collection, there has been much scholarship on the interface between law and literature since, some of which is noted below.

The relationship between law and literature has been approached from two angles. The less practiced and, for some, perhaps less interesting approach has been to study legal texts and to consider the literary forms which judges and lawyers employ in their work. Given the specialised nature of legal texts and the fact that, for the most part, they are inaccessible to the general public, this interest has remained within the professional legal community. The more common approach found in the books and extensive specialist journals has been to study literary texts and to focus on the question of how the law and justice are represented within the literature.

Law and literature scholarship has examined bodies of fiction as diverse as children's literature, the Canterbury Tales and gothic novels, and has included a focus on playwrights such as Shakespeare, Arthur Miller, Bertolt Brecht and Ibsen, and novelists such as Scott, Hardy, Edgar Allen Poe, J.G. Ballard and Angela Carter. This second and more common approach is of particular importance in the process of legal education. It examines literature to aid our understanding of law both within the legal community and outwith it. As some scholars have suggested, drawing on the insights of literature allows key legal issues to be brought to life in ways which orthodox legal materials cannot rival. It is worth doing because, like scholarship on Shakespeare, the Romantic Poets or French Realists, it may tell us something profound about human nature and human motivation. As one scholar put it:

> "literary texts are ... able to escape or smooth over strongly felt contradictions in belief and practice that other kinds of texts have difficulty dealing with. This can make them powerful instruments for 'solving' social and political problems ... or alternatively escaping the insufficiency in the face of such problems of other, supposedly more reality-orientated forms of discourse."[1]

This, then, is the promise and potential insight provided by scholarship on law and literature. It allows us, at its best, to contemplate such "contemporary" issues as consent, power and rape by looking afresh, for instance, at the relationship between Alec and Tess in *Tess of the D'Urbevilles* or the broader theme of violence against women. Discussions on the thin lines between anarchy, law and order and a police state can often be highlighted effectively through fictional characters and analysing their actions or themes like the impact of feminism. The work of Alice Walker in *The Color Purple* similarly provides an element of distance from people's own preconceptions and perspectives to allow debates on sensitive issues to be framed in a way by which people are likely to be less threatened. By looking through the eyes of characters, the issues are no less real but less personalised.

An overview of this scholarship reveals some key points to note. First, it demonstrates that there is a wealth of literary material and legal issues with which to engage. For some students and scholars, this approach to the study of law is hugely inspiring and liberating. However, at the same time, this body of work can be intimidating for others. The writing style encountered in some of the law and literature scholarship can be quite curious and the language rather murky. Reading some of the works is often akin to reading a difficult novel. They can certainly be challenging for students commencing their study of law.

Second, although a recent 2011 collection *Teaching Law and Literature* demonstrates an emerging diversity of literary material to analyse, including hip hop, graphic novels and comic strips, the tendency in this scholarship has been to focus on classical texts. The work of Homer,

Shakespeare, Dickens, Dostoevsky and Kafka feature as well as extensive reference to the Greek myths. This has the advantage of an assumed shared body of texts for scholars to discuss. At the same time, however, it has the disadvantage that many of the modern novels which students may have read dealing directly with law and justice issues do not generally feature. Following the upsurge in such popular fiction engendered by John Grisham and Scott Turow a whole host of authors have portrayed modern legal issues. These, however, have been largely ignored to date.

Related to the question of the selection of material, there is also the mundane but serious limitation of actually reading the literary texts. Unless one restricts oneself to a limited theme, or students are prepared to take a Stakhanovite approach to reading, there are boundaries to what can be achieved without the treatment of the material being either superficial or very narrow in its coverage. It is not feasible within an average undergraduate course to achieve any kind of grand overview of how law has been portrayed in literature. These issues of coverage are not insuperable but they point to why there might be less institutional impact of law and literature scholarship than the early progenitors might have hoped and it might be seen as marginalised.

Lastly, there does not appear to be any clear sign of any kind of work to link the scholarly interpretation of these books and plays with how the public perceive them and what impact the work might make on the behaviour of citizens. This potential for engagement into civil society is, however, an emerging feature behind recent developments in relation to the visual media. The temptation of academics to engage in obscure and ill-conceived debates remains in all fields, but the more recent excursions into the visual media seem to offer an alternative approach with greater potential for assessing the impact of the cultural products. It is to this topic that we now turn.

## LAW AND FILM

The emergence of an interest in law and film as a major focus in publishing terms has occurred since 1996 with some 18 books, 8 edited collections and 8 special journal issues on the topic. It seems clear that this is an area of scholarship with considerable potential. The rise in the study of film and law has a clear foundation stone: the assertion and perception that film influences how people see law and justice has been the fundamental notion that has inspired writers to explore a range of films. Looking at popular culture also stems from and complements concerns with the social construction of law and its socio-political nature—concerns which are found within traditional sociology of law and discussed in the chapters in this collection on empirical and critical approaches to the study of law. What has emerged, then, is a raft of work with both practical and intellectual concerns.

A major concern of the earlier law and film scholarship was to draw attention to how law was mis-portrayed in film as well as to use the visual media simply to capture the attention and interest of law students. Films can be shown which illustrate the operation of the legal system, both in terms of good practice as well as the potential for miscarriages of justice. The coverage of direct legal issues by the film industry, however, tends to focus on crime and more particularly murder. Hence large parts of the standard law degree syllabus have no films on which to draw. Nonetheless, the use of film as an illustrative teaching/pedagogic tool continues to be a worthwhile focus for lecturers and students alike. Such work has since been complemented by rather more ambitious attempts to use film's content to illustrate changes in the way social issues are treated and to explore who wields power in society. Film portrayals and the issues covered have been analysed to chart the rise of women lawyers, for instance, and the changes in the ways other oppressed groups have been treated. From *I am the Law* (1939) through *Adam's Rib* (1949) and *Jagged Edge* (1987) to *Legally Blonde* (2000), for example, we can see the changes in the visibility and role of women in the law.

Although scholarship on law and film is rather scarcer than its counterpart in law and literature, such material, whether utilised in individual doctrinal law classes, in courses on the philosophy or sociology of law, or in bespoke law and film courses, meets the need for a modern version of the rounded lawyer. There are, however, two developments which link law and popular culture with empirical approaches to legal study and to professional concerns and which provide much of the reason to believe that this visual media focus of modern law and popular culture is less likely to be marginalised within legal studies generally. First, there is the application to legal practice of the techniques of storytelling and rhetorical persuasion which can be observed in cinema. In much of Western legal culture the adversarial nature of the legal process involves the techniques of persuasion as much as technical legal knowledge. The ways in which both juries and lawyers understand the process of legal decision-making suggests that legal material is increasingly presented in cinematic terms. It is not just that juries expect the cases to resemble what they have seen on screen. Lawyers and judges themselves talk of deriving their role models within practice from fictional presentations of law. This interpenetration of reality and popular culture means that the scope of law and popular culture has moved beyond testing the fictional against the "real". The "real" is constructed by lawyers who tactically mould their arguments to fit into their audience's popular cultural expectations. This is done both in technological terms and in narrative terms. Juries are assisted by a range of audio-visual aids. In complex trials the issues are presented in the narrative forms with which the jury is familiar—that of the fictional film or TV trial. This development has important implications for the next generation of lawyers as well as for those with an interest from a theoretical angle on the representation of the law and its actors within popular culture and is important for the law school of the 21st century.

The second link which has made limited headway but which promises for the future is the attempt to link the ruminations of scholars on the likely impact of the media on people's behaviour with concrete empirical evidence. Rather than simply assuming that the media have an impact on behaviour and that this is why governments have always tried to censor what the people can see, there are now studies which seek to illustrate exactly how this occurs. Some law and film scholars look at how debates within law are conducted within film. This scholarship looks at how film shapes our expectations of law and justice in the world at large. In other words, how does law order our world through film? Jessica Silbey's suggestion that "film, *no less than law*, changes our perceptions of reality"[2] (my emphasis) captures the bedrock of interest in modern law and popular culture scholarship.

This approach to law and film has been driven by the widespread exposure of people in the 20th century to film. Assessing the impact of this exposure, however, is a far from easy task. Nonetheless, in the 21st century there have been a number of attempts to do just that. One team of international scholars conducted a study across six disparate jurisdictions on the ways in which law students derive their notions about justice and its relation to law. This revealed that the media, including films and TV, did indeed play a major role in the formation of ideas about justice and the legal system. Other studies on the impact of television alone, by way of contrast, have found it to be rather less than had been assumed. Although these are all limited studies, they do indicate the beginnings of a potentially valuable link between law and popular culture and empirical approaches to legal phenomena and, for instance, to examine critically the evidence rather than assume the existence of notions like the "CSI effect".

## LAW AND TV

In comparison to scholarship about law and film, work on law and television is less well-developed. There have been only two books and three collections of essays published on the subject, mostly on the representation of lawyers and legal processes within TV. The allure for many scholars of the rather more glamorous and seemingly prestigious world of cinema remains. However, a number of additional factors have also contributed to this relative paucity of television material at a time when scholarship on law and film has flourished. First of all, law on TV is exported less. Only a tiny fraction of the US lawyer dramas have ever been seen on British TV and vice-versa. Further, when TV drama focuses on legal issues, its subject-matter is usually policing or the prison system and not on the adjudication phase of law which occurs between these stages. Accordingly, lawyers and courts do not feature in the majority of law-related television dramas. In addition to legal dramas, of course, there is a range of other forms in which law and justice are represented on TV. For the last 50 years or so, for example, there have been "legal procedurals" set solely in the courtroom where we, the audience, act as the would-be jury. During the last 20 years there have also been legal reality shows where members of the public have their disputes adjudicated by TV "judges". However, for the most part, these are produced and consumed locally and work on analysing their significance has only started in the past two or three years. The question of actual televised justice is an issue which has yet to reach England, although there have been a couple of examples of television cameras entering Scottish courtrooms. The contrast with the availability of such material in the United States serves to emphasise the difficulties of replicating the kind of trans-national scholarship which has been such a feature of law and film. Additionally, it must be added, the mundane reality that television series occupy considerably more hours than individual films, as well as the older series often being unavailable for viewing, makes TV more challenging as a research subject than film.

The dearth of scholarship devoted to television as opposed to cinema in the law and popular culture field is, however, ironic. Television reaches the vast majority of the population. It was estimated that by the time a child in America in the 1980s had reached the age of 18 he/she would have been exposed to some 18,000 murders on television and that this would have shaped his/her outlook on law and order issues. The focus on crime-based series is one found in the rest of the world too and the schedules have actually increased the availability of this kind of material over the years. Television is more accessible in its production processes and distribution mechanism than is film. It provides news, dramas, documentaries and comedies 7 days a week, 24 hours a day. Cinema, the pre-eminent source of mass entertainment since the early 1920s, is on the decline. Visiting the cinema is now a luxury and is reserved for a relatively small population of Western audiences. The rise of television as the dominant source of entertainment and information, in light of the world's growing focus on the rule of law and international relations, demands consideration in the law and culture scholarship. The impact of the extension of access to visual material through laptops, tablets and phones will also require to be addressed. Just as the family visit to the cinema was replaced by the family sitting together round the TV, now the modern world of media available at anytime in any place demands the attention of scholars.

This is an issue which is beginning to be addressed. New scholarship analysing both the nature of the television product as well as its reception is developing, although the very different national contexts within which TV is produced requires careful examination. The impact, for instance, of the notion of "public service broadcasting" on the kinds of products made is worthy of investigation. More research on law and television, then, is needed to complement law school courses on law and literature, law and film, and law and popular culture more broadly. This work is likely to have the benefit of being seen as addressing the ever-present question of relevance with the concern over the impact of media on the behaviour of citizens.

CONCLUSION

The approach one takes to uncovering the nature of law depends crucially on the questions one wants answered. These in turn depend on who is making the inquiries and in what circumstances. The questions which a bright young student of law is likely to ask will usually be different from the immediate concerns of a lawyer representing poor or disadvantaged clients. Whereas the student may focus on the nature of justice and how it is achieved, the lawyer is more likely to be concerned with rather more mundane matters such as whether his or her client will be able to stay in their current accommodation. The lawyer will be aware that the big questions of the fairness of the system may have to wait for another day, irrespective of how important they may actually be in determining, for instance, that minority ethnic applicants rarely achieve success before particular judges. The broader social context, too, is highly important. It may be that not having money denies people access to proper advice and representation. It may also be the case that being of a certain sex, ethnicity or sexuality is known or thought to affect one's chances before the law, either in terms of the way the rules are applied or enforced. So, taking all this into account, it should be clear that the study of law does not take place in some kind of vacuum in which people opt to become "doctrinal" lawyers or "empirical" lawyers or "philosophical lawyers". How someone studies law is more a question of teasing out what approach best serves one's immediate purpose.

The overarching concern of many legal scholars has been to uncover how it is that a legal system which promises so much in terms of equal treatment, so consistently operates in the interests of the few against the interests of the many. Equally, their concern is with why this is either not known about or has been allowed to happen without greater social conflict arising. It is to answer questions like this that scholars have asked not just questions about the impact of particular sets of rules but, more importantly, what contribution is made to this situation by the way law is represented in books, films and on television. The point about law and popular culture is that it takes us into a realm of enterprise which legal scholars have, as yet, ventured only in a very limited way. It completes the circle of enquiry about how law and justice really operate. It looks not just at the actions and practices of the justice system, but at what factors help to drive the success or failure of laws and legal systems. By taking seriously the culture of law in the form in which the system is presented to the public, it can help give a richer picture than previously available. It is not ever likely to be the dominant approach to legal study, but it provides rich possibilities to complement other scholarly work.

Popular culture, of course, is not some static entity but is constantly evolving. Some areas such as gaming have yet to be addressed but are also of potential significance in all these debates. Gauging the impact of *Phoenix Wright, Ace Attorney* and his struggles in the Nintendo interactive courtroom dramas on the perceptions of the world's youth regarding law and justice is something that has yet to be undertaken. It may, however, be the future.

## FURTHER READING

Aristodemou, Mària, *Law and Literature* (Oxford: Oxford University Press, 2000).

Freeman, Michael (ed), *Law and Popular Culture* (Oxford: Oxford University Press, 2005).

Greenfield, Steve, Osborn, Guy and Robson, Peter, *Film and the Law: the cinema of justice* (Oxford: Hart, 2010).

Kamir, Orit, *Framed: Women in Law and Film* (Durham, North Carolina: Duke University Press, 2006).

Robson, Peter and Silbey, Jessica (eds), *Law and Justice on the Small Screen* (Oxford: Hart, 2012).

Thornton, Margaret (ed), *Romancing the Tomes: popular culture, law and feminism* (London: Cavendish, 2002).

---

[1] Faller, L., Crime and Defoe: a new kind of writing (Cambridge: Cambridge University Press, 1993) [cited in Morison, J. and Bell, C. (eds), Tall Stories? Reading Law and Literature (Aldershot: Dartmouth, 1996), p.1].

[2] Silbey, J., "Truth Tales and Trial Films" (2007) 40 LOY. L.A. L. Rev. 551.

# 6. HISTORICAL APPROACHES

*T.T. Arvind*

"[L]egal history is the study of legal change. Unless we regard law as no more than a body of randomly changing rules, its history must be an essential dimension in its study."[1]

Thus wrote Sir John Baker in his inaugural lecture in 1998. Yet it is not necessarily obvious to a law student—or, for that matter, a practising lawyer—why it should be so. After all, to return to an analogy from Chapter 1, plumbers do not typically spend their time studying 19th century plumbing techniques, or researching the history of butterfly valves. What is it about *law* that makes studying its history such an important part of learning the law?

That is the question to which this chapter turns. The answer, as we will see, is both straightforward and compelling. At the most basic level, the study of the history of the law, and of the law's place in the history of a community, brings together virtually all the themes and approaches you have looked at in the other chapters of this book, and is therefore a worthy intellectual endeavour in its own right. Tracing the origins of legal doctrines can be extremely challenging in intellectual terms, involving considerable detective work and the study of materials that, not infrequently, nobody has studied before. The ultimate results of historical study can be fascinating in terms of the links they reveal, be it the question of why England developed a system where offers to purchase houses are not binding, or the relationship between the Black Death and the ancestor of the modern tort of negligence.

But the importance of legal history to understanding the law goes far beyond uncovering the origins of legal rules. Much more fundamentally, legal history is important because of what we can learn about the nature of law itself by looking at the historical origins of legal rules and concepts, and the processes by which they came to have the meaning and significance they do today. Legal history confronts us squarely with the fact that the law as we know it today is contingent. Many of the principles and ideas we hold to be fundamental to our legal system have not always been part of the law. Their role within the legal system is, rather, in no small part a product of the manner in which different persons chose to deal with the challenges and problems thrown up by social and economic change in times past. Analysing how the legal system worked before what we today consider its "fundamental" principles had come into existence can tell us much of interest about the role these principles actually play within the legal system.

Further, as legal history also demonstrates, the relationship between legal and social change does not only run one way, and judges and legislators are not the only agents of legal change. Historical work has thrown considerable light on the manner in which ordinary people deal with the law, on the extent to which their responses to changing conditions are influenced by the ideals of justice and legality the law is said to embody, and on how the strategies they devise to cope with or take advantage of legal rules influence the long term path of the law. All of these have contributed significantly to our understanding of the position of law in society.

However, these insights are important not just for the light they can shed on the manner and extent to which the development of the law influences and is influenced by social, political and intellectual forces within the broader community, but also for the light they shed on the structure and functioning of the modern legal system. As we will see in this chapter, the result of engaging with the insights of legal history is a richer and far more nuanced understanding of the law itself, its strengths and shortcomings, and why it is the way it is.

In this chapter we will start by setting out what is distinctive about legal history, and how it relates to other types of legal scholarship. We will then examine, in brief, the methods and frameworks that legal historians use to study the law, and conclude by looking at what the historical approach can tell us about law itself.

## WHAT IS LEGAL HISTORY?

Rather than starting by describing what legal history is, it is useful to start by describing what it is not. Legal history is not the bare study of older cases and statutes. All lawyers engage with historical sources, and do so far more frequently than their counterparts in many other disciplines. Most of you will, when you study the law of contract, come across *Pinnel's Case*,[2] a decision from 1602 which is still seen as an important authority in relation to the effect of part payment of debts. It is also not uncommon to see lawyers and academics relying on cases from the 18th and 19th centuries in support of propositions they seek to establish. A 2008 decision of the House of Lords turned in part on the meaning of a phrase used by Lord Mansfield in a case from 1774,[3] and the recent academic attempts to develop an account of the law of "unjust enrichment"—adverted to in Chapter 1—drew not inconsiderable inspiration (and authority) from *Moses v Macfarlane*,[4] a case decided in 1760. Equally, academics, theorists and practitioners dissatisfied with their contemporary laws have for centuries appealed to older cases or practices as examples of a more refined, principled approach from which the law has since fallen away and to which it must be restored.

This is not how legal historians view the past of the law. As the examples cited above suggest, lawyers operating within a practical or doctrinal context rather than treating their materials as *historical* sources tend to treat them as a resource that can be drawn upon to generate principles, concepts and rules that help us deal with modern day issues. In this tradition older cases, much like modern cases, are sources of authority that tell us what the law is or how it is applied, and that can be used to construct legal arguments and legal doctrine as long as they continue to represent good law, notwithstanding their age. To take an example, the fact that *Pinnel's case* was decided over 400 years ago, in very different social and economic conditions, is rarely mentioned in textbook discussions of this case—it is treated as an authority for the rule it established in exactly the same way as a case decided last year.

A legal historian, in contrast, is not principally concerned with the meaning an old case or statute could have for people of our day. The principal concern of a legal historian is, instead, the meaning which they actually had for the people of their time. It is far from uncommon to find that a legal principle, case or statute was understood in a range of different ways, or carried a range of meanings and significances for the many different groups of people who were within its orbit. In such circumstances, the legal historian—unlike the doctrinal or philosophical lawyer—does not aim to select the "best" meaning for the law, but to document and account for these differences. The aim of legal history, from this perspective, is to reconstruct how people thought about and worked with the law in the time period being studied.

Legal history is often said to have two aspects, the internal and the external. Internal legal history seeks to reconstruct the manner in which lawyers or jurists thought about the law. Internal legal history is, therefore, principally concerned with the law itself, as it would have been recognised by jurists of the time—encompassing legal sources, concepts, rules, and the theoretical and analytical frameworks that jurists used to turn a disparate mass of cases into a more or less consistent body of law. External legal history, or "law and history" as it is sometimes also called, in contrast is concerned with reconstructing the social life of the law in a given period. How did the law affect social, economic and political life in that period? How did people respond to the law and work with the law? How did the social, economic and political concerns of the day affect the development of the law? The focus of external legal history on such questions means that it is sometimes said to study the "law in action", and to aim at reconstructing how people affected by the law (and not just lawyers) thought about and worked with the law. To this extent, legal history has much in common with the empirical approaches to law discussed in Chapter 3.

Legal historians of all stripes place legal change at the heart of what they study. It is because the past of the law was different that a historical understanding of the law cannot be grounded in the categories, concepts and assumptions of the modern law. The law of any period must, instead, be understood on its own terms, with reference to the categories and assumptions that people of that period would have brought to bear in thinking about the law. An important consequence of this is that legal history is explanatory rather than justificatory. Many modern theorists, particularly those inclined to doctrinal or philosophical approaches, see the point of what they do as being to analyse justifications for legal rules, that is, to examine whether a particular legal rule is justifiable on the basis of a particular theoretical, moral or philosophical framework. Where the precise scope or content of a legal rule is uncertain, they seek to find the "best" rule, by which they mean the most justifiable rule. Legal history in contrast seeks to *explain* why legal rules are the way they are (or were they way they were) by studying the process of change. Just as it does not seek to resolve uncertainties as to the law that people of that era would have perceived, it also does not seek to come up with *justifications* as to why particular legal rules are good or just. The aim of legal history is to study the nature and effect of the legal doctrine of ages past, not to contribute to its development. This aim, and the attention that is consequently paid to the context of legal change, give legal history its distinctiveness, and set it apart from other ways of engaging with the past of law. Legal history is thus distinguished both by the questions with which it is concerned, and by the methods it uses to address those questions.

Nevertheless, legal history and other modes of studying of the law are not separate worlds. In recent years, there has been considerable cross-fertilisation between the two. For example, A.W. Brian Simpson's *Leading Cases in the Common Law*,[5] and the more focused "Landmark Cases" series it inspired, contain a collection of papers, each of which examines a specific "leading" case against the backdrop of its historical and social context. Similarly, a number of legal theorists have in recent years used historical materials and historical arguments to shed new light (usually a critical light) on legal rules, concepts and doctrine. We will return to the intertwining of legal history with other modes of analysis in the concluding section. First, however, we will look in some detail at the methods legal historians use to investigate the law.

## THE PRACTICE OF LEGAL HISTORY

Studying the past of the law on its own terms is harder than it sounds. The question of what the law was at a particular point of time is an empirical question. A legal historian does not have the option of constructing an argument as to what the law can arguably be said to be, as doctrinal scholars frequently do. A legal historian must, instead, determine what a lawyer in that period would have understood the law as being. This is a question of fact, not one of formulating the best argument. It means that historians must, if necessary, be prepared to admit that they are unable to determine what the law at a particular point of time was, either because we do not have enough material to find out, or because the law at the time was genuinely unclear, so that a lawyer in that period would not have been quite certain what the law was.

A complicating factor is the nature of historical sources. In the context of the modern legal system, we are used to having a plethora of published and readily accessible materials we can use to understand the law. Go back as little as two centuries, however, and the picture changes radically. A person trying to understand the modern law of contract (for example) would probably start with a textbook on contract law. But in 1812, there were no legal textbooks in the modern sense—they would not start being written until the middle of that century. A small number of treatises, written for practitioners, existed, but being written for practitioners they assume that their reader starts off with at least some understanding of the law. There were also no law reports in the modern sense in 1812. The modern series of law reports prepared by the Incorporated Council of Law Reporting did not start being published until 1865. The reports that do exist from earlier periods are variable in relation to their quality and reliability. Some are excellent but many are not. Many reports originated as a lawyer's notebooks, kept for his personal use, and as we go further back the focus of reports is increasingly on pleading rather than what we would today consider the substance of the law. Equally, the quantity of published material is dwarfed by the sheer mass of material that remains in manuscript form, scattered across libraries in England, North America and elsewhere in the common law world (although this is changing as the most important sources are released on microfilm, microfiche or digitally).

A lawyer who studies legal history must therefore work with very different types of sources from those with which students of the modern law are familiar, not all of which are well documented and many of which will never have been read or analysed in detail. Much of what you will read in legal history is, for example, based on primary archival research— whether it be the official records of the courts and government departments preserved in the National Archives, or the collections of documents preserved in the libraries of the Inns of Court, or documents in special collections in libraries or even in private hands. Equally, historical accounts are frequently based on the study of a wider range of documents than is usual in doctrinal research. Cases and legislation generated public excitement in the past much as they do now, and much information on the operation of the law, or on legal debates, or even on leading cases can be gathered by looking at contemporary literature, news sources, Parliamentary debates, records of organisations such as chambers of commerce or labour associations, or popular writing.

This gives considerable room for creativity in research and makes legal history a stimulating area of work because there is always new knowledge waiting to be uncovered. Often, legal historians are able to shed considerable light on an aspect of the law simply by looking at a different type of source. For example, Robert B. Stevens, in his book *The Independence of the Judiciary: The View from the Lord Chancellor's Office*[6] set out a fresh and very different perspective on the important constitutional question of what "judicial independence" means, by examining not case law but the records of the Lord Chancellor's Office and analysing what they could tell us about the interaction between the executive and the judiciary. Similarly, legal historians who examine the law in action have uncovered much of interest about the law by looking at things to do with social or economic history, ranging from the records of banks or insurers, to statistics on railway fatalities, to public reaction to the failure of dams, and drawing links between these and the law. Thus, for example, it has been argued that the changes in the law in relation to accidents in the workplace in the 19th century were at least partially influenced by judges' awareness of the growing importance of commercial activity in society, and the consequent need not to interfere with enterprise.

But it will not suffice to simply analyse a broad range of sources using a modern framework. If we want to understand the past on its own terms, we must, as we have seen, start by putting to one side the concepts and categories we use to think about the law and instead begin to use the concepts and categories that a person of that period would have used to think about the law. The further back we go, the more different and unfamiliar these categories become. Returning to our example of the law of contract, let us go a further two hundred years back from 1812. In 1612, where we have now arrived, the very idea of a "law of contract" would have been unintelligible to many English lawyers. It is not that contracts did not exist—they did, and were commonly used—but they were not an organising category within the law. Rather (and simplifying somewhat), they were seen as tools for transferring rights and organising relations within the categories that existed.

It is not just the categories that change. The sources from which we derive the law have undergone several changes. Today, we see cases and legislation as being the main sources of the law, but as John Baker has shown, a lawyer in 1612 would have seen what was then called "comen erudition"—or common learning—as an important source of the law which was in some ways even more important than case law.[7] This is even more true of analytical and theoretical frameworks. David Ibbetson has shown that for much of the 19th century, natural law provided the bulk of the theoretical framework within which most lawyers—including judges, treatise-writers and practitioners—thought about the law.[8] A mere hundred years later, it is hard to find any trace of this framework outside a narrow segment of legal theory.

How, then, do we discover what categories and frameworks were used in a given period? Legal historians, typically, work by consulting a broad range of sources. Much has been learnt about the law in late mediaeval and early modern England by looking at surviving records of "Readings" in the Inns of Court—essentially, the sixteenth century equivalent of undergraduate lecture notes. Attention must also be paid to the social context, even in internal legal history. S.F.C. Milsom, a leading 20th century legal historian, famously argued that it was impossible to understand the law of 12th century England without understanding the 12th century feudal environment in which the law operated. Even so, the task is not always easy, particularly when it comes to reconstructing the different theoretical and analytical frameworks that people used to organise the law. These frameworks are particularly subject to change, and are particularly prone to being unwritten and undocumented. Legal historians therefore often have to work with circumstantial evidence, and have to be alert to the possibility that there may not have been any consensus in society on these frameworks at a given point of time, much as there is very little consensus today in relation to the theoretical or conceptual basis of the law of tort.

These tasks are complicated by the challenge posed by the documentary nature of legal history. All legal history is derived from documentary evidence. But, as some historians have long argued and as work in legal history has demonstrated, we cannot always assume that written sources are neutral or accurate, even when these sources are official records. An example is provided by a recent piece by Shannon McSheffrey,[9] which examines an ostensibly simple and straightforward legal record from fifteenth century England—the record of the annulment of a marriage in the Consistory court of the diocese of London in 1469. Through a careful analysis of other surrounding documentation, such as the wills of two of the protagonists, she demonstrates how the Consistory records probably represent a false suit, covering over what was possibly a far more troubling series of events. Working with legal history can, in this sense, resemble a detective enterprise as much as it resembles an empirical enterprise, where we are required to hunt down the evidence, piece together a complete story from disparate pieces of evidence, and also to assess the reliability, veracity and accuracy of each piece of evidence. Many legal historians therefore follow mainstream historians in treating the less well-supported portions of their historical findings as provisional or temporary, on the basis that further evidence may subsequently emerge which poses a challenge to them. This does not, of course, apply to all of legal history—there is much in legal history of which we can be very certain—but it is something that must always be kept in mind when studying the past of the law.

THE PURSUIT OF LEGAL HISTORY

Having seen what legal history is about and what legal historians do, let us now return to the question with which we began. Why is the pursuit of legal history worthwhile? What does it tell us about the law, and why do its findings matter? There are a range of answers that could be given to these questions. In this section, I focus on three responses which are of particular relevance to an undergraduate student learning the law.

First, legal history *integrates* the law by bringing together many of the concerns and methods of the other strands of studying the law. Most obviously, legal history incorporates many elements of doctrinal and sociological perspectives, because the "sociology of the past" and the doctrine of the past are its primary concerns. Legal history, as we have seen, is also empirical. It shares the curiosity about the creation, implementation, use and social effect of the law that, as you have seen in Chapter 3, characterises empirical work. Whilst its methods are neither qualitative nor quantitative, they nevertheless share the overriding concern with evidence and the interpretation of data that also characterises empirical work. At the same time, legal history is also comparative. The past, as we have seen, is a different country, and when we visit the law as it was in the past, we see familiar-sounding concepts and doctrines in an unfamiliar context, often with an unfamiliar content. Legal history draws our attention to similarities and differences, and to continuities and change, in much the same way and with much the same salutary effects as comparative law does. At the same time, to the extent that the history of the law is at least in part an intellectual history, it also reflects philosophical perspectives on the law. The result is that legal history is intrinsically oriented towards giving us an understanding of how the insights into the law afforded by the different approaches this book discusses fit together in creating a complete picture of the law.

Secondly, history *humanises* the law by bringing out the stories in the background to the cases and legal rules that are usually studied as abstract principles. Legal historians are, of course, not the only ones who seek to do this. Feminist theorists and socio-legal theorists have also done so quite extensively, sometimes even using the methods of historical inquiry discussed in the preceding section. But legal history, through its study of the impact of legal rules upon people, and the manner in which people respond to legal rules, draws our attention to the fact that law is never just a top-down enterprise of formulating and applying relatively abstract rules and principles. It is a human enterprise, which is defined as much by the interaction between these rules and society as it is by the rules themselves. People subject to the law frequently attempt, sometimes successfully, to reshape the functioning of the law through the way in which they react to it. Shannon McSheffrey, in the study discussed in the previous section, shows how ordinary people for a brief period successfully exploited procedural and evidentiary aspects of litigation before the Consistory court to obtain results—divorces where marriages had broken down—that were quite contrary to the law as it then existed. Examples of this sort abound in the past and the present of the law. In studying these, legal history like more sociological or empirical approaches to the law points to the importance of a study and understanding of the law that is broader than the mere learning of legal rules.

Thirdly, and most importantly, legal history *contextualises* the law, by bringing to the fore the complex debates and considerations that go into its making. In your study of tort law, you will come across the case of *Rylands v Fletcher*,[10] a case from 1868 involving the question of liability for escape of water from a burst industrial reservoir. The rule in that case assumes a somewhat different colour when we take into account the fact that the defendant in that case was one of the most prominent industrialists in England, employing over 12,000 persons in his various mills, and that the case came at a time when there was a lot of anxiety about the safety of water storage, following a number of high-profile failures of dams and reservoirs.[11] The same is true of other developments in the common law, whether through cases or statutes, as the leading cases series and corresponding work in relation to statutes has shown. By focusing on the context of the law, and on the pressures and attitudes that produce legal change, legal history shows the law at its best and its worst, and thus gives us an acute sense of the strengths and weaknesses of the legal system.

Further, the fact that broader social concerns and pressures have influenced many important legal developments suggests that the law is not just changing but also *contingent* in the manner in which it changes. As we saw in the previous section, it is not just superficial or detailed aspects of the law that change. Fundamental principles of the law, its goals and its structure also change, and these changes are in important part influenced both by the social circumstances to which the law is responding and the manner in which these circumstances are translated into the language and theoretical structure of the law. While the direction of change is unpredictable, it is not random, and it is therefore usually capable of explanation.

The contingent nature of legal change comes to fullest prominence in external legal history, but also animates many works of internal legal history. The ability of legal history to shed light on why the law changed in the way it did has seen some of the most fruitful and controversial interaction between the domains of legal history and legal theory. In the latter half of the twentieth century, a number of scholars used historical analysis to attempt to show that rules which legal theorists celebrate and justify on moral grounds today were not prompted by the moral considerations that are thought to justify them, but by other social, historical and economic factors. The best known of these are Morton Horwitz's account of the impact of free market principles upon the development of law in the United States[12] and Patrick Atiyah's history of the rise of contract law from the late 18th century.[13] Of a different import, albeit in a similarly contextualist vein, is Bruce Kercher's study of how the colonial environment of the New South Wales penal colony influenced the manner in which the common law developed in Australia, and in particular the way its values and rules diverged from those of the common law of England.[14] Atiyah's and Horwitz's texts were critical, taking aim at doctrines and principles in the modern law that the authors argued lacked the justification or purpose customarily assigned to them. Both have been criticised, but they nevertheless illustrate the importance of legal history to legal theory. Their aim was to provide us with insight into the values that law embodies, and how it came to chose those values over other competing values it could have chosen. This is a question that is of obvious importance to understanding our legal system, and it is a question only legal history can fully answer.

This brings us to a final point, which is an appropriate conclusion to this brief survey of legal history. Let us return to the quote with which this chapter began. Baker, in emphasising the indispensability of legal history, was responding to the suggestion that legal history was becoming "less relevant to a student's needs". Even if legal history does not enjoy the prominence on the undergraduate legal curriculum that legal theory or legal doctrine do, the importance of legal history, Baker argued, lies in "keeping alive an understanding of the laws of England in a rapidly changing world". The legal historian does this by uncovering the foundations of those laws, and by shedding light on the processes that have led from those foundations to the structures and edifices that today comprise our legal system. Through doing so, legal history gives us a far richer understanding of the nature, shape and doctrines of our legal system. For this reason, a study of the historical background of the law is, and will long remain, an essential part of learning the law.

## FURTHER READING

Baker, J.H., *An Introduction to English Legal History*, 4th edn (Oxford: Oxford University Press, 2002).

Cornish, W.R., and Clark, G. de N., *Law and Society in England: 1750–1950* (London: Sweet and Maxwell, 1989).

Milsom, S.F.C., *Historical Foundations of the Common Law*, 2nd edn (Oxford: Oxford University Press, 1981).

Ibbetson, D., "What is Legal History a History Of?" (2003) 6 *Current Legal Issues* 33.

Phillips, J., "Why Legal History Matters" (2010) 41 Vict Univ of Wellington L Rev 293.

---

[1]  J.H. Baker, "Why the History of English Law Has not Been Finished" (2000) 59 C.L.J. 62.

[2]  (1602) 5 Co. Rep. 117a.

[3]  The case in question is *R (Bancoult) v Secretary of State for Foreign and Commonwealth Affairs* [2008] UKHL 61; [2009] 1 A.C. 453, where one of the issues related to the meaning and effect of the decision of Lord Mansfield in *Campbell v Hall* (1774) 1 Cowp 204, 98 E.R. 1045.

[4]  (1760) 2 Burr 1005; 97 E.R. 676. Coincidentally enough, this was also a decision of Lord Mansfield.

[5]  A.W. Brian Simpson, *Leading Cases in the Common Law* (Oxford: Oxford University Press, 1996).

[6]  Robert B. Stevens, *The Independence of the Judiciary: The View from the Lord Chancellor's Office* (Oxford: Clarendon Press, 1997).

[7]  J.H. Baker, "The Inns of Court and Legal Doctrine" in T.M. Charles-Edwards, M.E. Owen and D.B. Walters (eds), *Lawyers and Laymen: Studies in the History of the Law presented to Professor Dafydd Jenkins* (Cardiff: University of Wales Press, 1986).

[8]  D.J. Ibbetson, "Natural Law and Common Law" (2001) 5 *Edinburgh Law Review 5*.

[9]  Shannon McSheffrey, "Detective Fiction in the Archives: Court Records and the Uses of Law in Late Mediaeval England" (2008) 65 *History Workshop Journal* 65.

[10]  (1868) L.R. 3 H.L. 330.

[11]  See, in particular, the analysis in A.W. Brian Simpson, "Legal Liability for Bursting Reservoirs: The Historical Context of *Rylands v Fletcher*" (1984) 13 J. Legal Studies 209.

[12]  Morton J. Horwitz, *The Transformation of American Law*, 1780–1860 (Cambridge, MA: Harvard University Press, 1977).

[13]  P.S. Atiyah, *The Rise and Fall of Freedom of Contract* (Oxford: Oxford University Press 1985).

[14]  Bruce Kercher, *An Unruly Child: A History of Law in Australia* (Sydney: Allen and Unwin, 1995).

# 7. COMPARATIVE APPROACHES

*Prue Vines*

## INTRODUCTION

The study of comparative law sounds fascinating, and it is. Not all legal systems are the same and we can learn a great deal about our own system by studying those of others. The comparative study of law cuts across many of the other approaches to legal study explored in this book. So, as we shall see, comparative law connects in various ways with doctrinal, historical, empirical and philosophical approaches to the study of law. All of this makes it a rich and exciting subject of enquiry.

Merely describing other systems of law is not quite the same thing as comparative legal research, although gathering some of that information may be part of what the comparative lawyer does. Although the comparative lawyer works by comparing legal systems or legal concepts, this is not as simple a process as it sounds. Just as words in languages rarely have exactly equivalent meaning in other languages, legal concepts and structures rarely have exact equivalents in other legal systems. This means that to take a comparative approach to studying law requires something more than merely describing concepts in the compared systems that appear at first glance to have the same function or role. A deeper analysis is required in order to ensure that like is really being compared with like.

Comparative law is the study of the legal systems or legal concepts of different countries (or groups of countries) on a systematic basis. It can also be thought of as the study of the relationships between these various legal systems. Within legal systems a comparative lawyer will also consider the relationships between the rules and the legal system itself. It is common to find comparative lawyers examining a particular aspect of law across various jurisdictions. So, for example, comparative constitutional law or comparative obligations law might be the object of study. Context is also important, so that the history of a legal system, and countries' economies and social structures will usually be important for the comparative lawyer to consider.

In this chapter we set out the major concepts and concerns of comparative law, hoping that this will encourage you to find out more about this interesting approach to legal study. The chapter examines the approaches and methods of comparative legal research, as well as considering what comparative law is useful for. The answer to this second (and more important) question is that comparative legal research is useful for very many reasons. But we begin our look at comparative legal research by going back to its foundations and exploring its original preoccupation: the classifying of legal systems.

## CLASSIFYING LEGAL SYSTEMS

Early attempts at comparative legal study often operated as "mapping exercises" aimed at classification—assigning various countries' laws to particular categories or "families" of legal system. Indeed, one of the major projects of comparative law has been to ask, "What is a legal system?" and "What is a legal tradition?" and then to study in a comparative way the systems or traditions found. The simplest way to conceive of a legal system is to think of a country and its legal operation including its constitutional and administrative arrangements. That is a narrow conception of a legal system. A broader view, however, conceives of a legal system as including the way in which lawyers reason, the techniques of the law and its institutions. These features might be shared by a number of countries. When we think of legal systems in this way we are referring to "parent legal families" and we are carrying out a process of classification. In order to fit a country's legal system into such a classification one would normally have to consider its history and development, its dominant mode of thought, its institutions and personnel, and what it sees as the sources of law. So, for example, German and Italian law are regarded as part of the same parent family of civil law systems. They are each unique, but there are similarities in their history, ways of thinking, sources of law and so on, which make it meaningful to see them as part of a larger group.

One way of thinking of parent legal families is in terms of families of origin. So, for example, families of legal systems include: common law (derived from England); civil law (derived from the Roman law as it applied in Europe), the former socialist legal systems (derived from the Union of Soviet Socialist Republics) and chthonic law (sometimes referred to as Indigenous laws or customary laws). Other ways of classifying laws depend more on the traditions or inspiration of each one—for example, Western laws (including common law and civil law); Chinese and Japanese law, Muslim law, (former) Soviet law, Hindu law, chthonic traditions (traditions such as Aboriginal Australian law which is characterised by a close relationship with the land).

This brings us to the question of what sort of criteria should be used to organise such classifications. What makes a legal tradition? A legal tradition is much more than a set of laws. The word "tradition" is used to encompass the cultural norms, the political, economic context and the connections to previous laws by history and geography. A legal tradition gives rise to a set of cultural attitudes to law which is profoundly important to the operation of the law within it. Sometimes the term "legal culture" is used instead of "legal tradition". For example, in Scotland the legal tradition encompasses not only the rules themselves, but also attitudes about how rules should operate, the relationship of Scotland with England and the rest of the world, attitudes about how the criminal law should interact with private law and so on. Scotland itself is interesting because its law links the two great legal traditions of Europe (the common law and the Roman/civil law) making it what is known as a "hybrid" legal system. This illustrates the pluralistic nature of the idea of legal traditions. They can overlap and there can be multiple allegiances.

**An example—characterising civil law and common law systems**
It is useful for students to have some familiarity with the characteristics which are regarded as differentiating the two largest groups of legal families or traditions in the world: the common law tradition and the civil law tradition. It is important to recognise that these are "ideal types" and that many countries' versions of civil or common law may not conform in all respects to these descriptions. Nevertheless, it may be useful to compare the two in a table:

|  | Civil Law | Common Law |
|---|---|---|
| **Some countries using this system** | France, Germany, Italy, Switzerland, Japan | England, Canada, USA, Australia, New Zealand, India, Nigeria, Kenya, Singapore |
| **Origins** | Roman law *via* Bologna 12th century | English law from Anglo-Saxon times |
| **Procedure in court** | Inquisitorial (judge is in charge of the action and directs pre-trial action, trial may be in a series of meetings) | Adversarial (parties are in charge of the action, usually there is a single session trial, judge is unfamiliar with action before trial) |
|  | No jury | Jury |
| **Training** | Trained as judge/ lawyer/advocate from the beginning | Trained as lawyers, then judges selected from lawyers, especially advocates |
| **Role of judge** | Less important | Very important |
| **Sources of law** | Codes, academic writings, legislation | Cases (judge-made law), legislation |
| **Legal reasoning** | General to particular, often highly abstract, emphasis on rules | Analogy, pragmatic, concrete, emphasis on parties, use of the doctrine of precedent |
| **Distinctive institutions** | Unjustified enrichment; regulation of everyday matters e.g., names; a substantive private/ public law distinction | The trust, agency, consideration for contract, estoppels |

It is vital that this table is not seen as showing that the civil law and common law systems are reducible to these elements. However, some of these elements help us compare the two systems or families of law. The origins of the civil law is from the Roman laws of Justinian as they had been "glossed"—annotated or commented on—by scholars in the first millennium. The University of Bologna in the 12th century was the basis of a revival in this sort of scholarship and ultimately most of the countries of Europe used a mixture of this law with their own background tribal or other law. By contrast, common law originated in England, derived from the Anglo-Saxon laws as affected by the Normans. In turn, the colonial history of the countries of Europe affected the development of their legal systems. The legal system of the former colony often reflects its coloniser so that, for example, Australia, being colonised by the British, became a common law country, and Argentina, having been colonised by Spain, became a civil law country. Some countries which were never colonised, such as Japan, simply chose what they thought was best—it chose to become a civil law country.

Common law is often characterised as having adversarial systems and contrasted with civil law systems which are seen as inquisitorial. The difference between the inquisitorial and adversarial system is to some extent explained by the development of the jury in the common law. Because everything had to happen in front of the jury, the common law trial became a one-session "show" or "contest", whereas where there was no jury in the civil systems it was possible to determine legal questions in a more piecemeal way, over several meetings until the judge was satisfied. (Of course, France adopted the jury in the 19th century—just another example of how the paradigmatic elements of legal systems are often departed from).

A major difference between the two traditions is the conception of the judge—in the common law system the judge is a resplendent and imposing figure, a law-giver, and generally he or she has been appointed from amongst the advocates or barristers at the bar. The judge is much less significant in the civilian systems and has generally been educated all along as a judge, being somewhat more like a civil servant. He or she is not regarded as making law. The sources of law are also different. Because the civil systems use Codes which are often highly abstract, much of the legal reasoning of the judges is done by deducing from the abstract law whether it applies to a case before it. The case does not make new law. By contrast, in common law legal reasoning the rule from a case which has similar facts and is higher in the same hierarchy will determine the outcome, and a case decision may change the law. That is, the cases themselves, as determined by judges, make the law. This is the doctrine of precedent which reflects the fact that judges make law within a tradition which confines them and prevents arbitrariness.

The way law is classified into various legal subjects within the two systems differs as well. Common law as a system in many jurisdictions includes equity as a somewhat separate body of law developed from the historical position of the Chancellor as the person who took petitions for the

King. This body of law is seen as entirely distinct in some common law jurisdictions. In others, such as the United States, the different constructs of equity, such as the trust, are seen as swimming within the larger general sea of the law. In Australia, which takes the strictest view of this, the equity jurisdiction and the common law jurisdiction are regarded as two streams which flow together but do not mingle. The civil law systems do not have equity as a body of law; in particular the trust as it is recognised in Anglo-American law does not exist there.

BEYOND CLASSIFICATION

The danger with classification into legal families, as you will already be aware, is that within these legal families individual legal systems vary markedly. For example, as we have already seen, not all civil law systems have no juries. Equally, not all common law systems maintain juries in every trial. Many systems mix up elements. In both England and Australia, for example, (both common law systems) the coronial jurisdiction (which determines whether a death is suspicious) is inquisitorial rather than adversarial.

More significantly, however, classifying systems into legal families only tells us a minimum amount about the legal system. Contemporary comparative legal research has moved beyond classification and now asks more probing questions. This, however, has made the exercise more challenging. Classification questions such as "What is this legal system like?" and "How is it different from that one?" might be relatively straightforward to answer at the level we explored above. But if one asks a question like "How do these legal systems deal with the concept of causation?" then the answer becomes more complex and potentially quite philosophical. Comparative legal research has gradually come to acknowledge the cultural characteristics which affect legal systems, their operations and the meaning of legal concepts within particular legal systems. Ultimately, what is important for comparative lawyers is the law as it operates in its context—the law in action. Comparative lawyers might ask how different legal systems manage one particular issue—for example, how do France, Japan and England deal with motor car accidents? Or, how are certain personnel dealt with, for example, judges? Of these two examples, the conceptual boundary of "motor car accidents" seems more obvious than that of "judges". But any boundaries can be extremely difficult to draw because the legal systems themselves may define "motor car accidents" or "judges" differently. This raises the question of the extent to which the researcher is comparing like with like. For example, does "motor car accidents" include accidents involving bicycles or accidents involving pedestrians or farm vehicles in each jurisdiction being compared? Similarly "judge" may mean different things in different systems. Indeed, what counts as "law" may be problematic in itself. It is only relatively recently that Aboriginal law has been recognised as law by non-Aboriginals in Australia. Earlier it was often regarded as "folklore" or "religion". This demonstrates the difficulties of comparing traditions and how the more different the cultures are, the more difficult the comparative exercise may be. Comparative lawyers have also come to accept that legal systems are dynamic. This means that a historical perspective is equally important to the process of comparative legal research. So questions in comparative law might also include whether all legal systems go through similar stages and whether there is a causal connection between the development of one legal system and the content of another. The challenge for comparative legal research is that both the basic and the deeper levels of questions and answers are needed to have a fully developed comparative law analysis, making it at times a difficult, though always rewarding enterprise.

## APPROACHES AND METHODS

The question of what scholarship amounts properly to comparative legal research is a constant debate within the community of scholars who describe themselves as comparative lawyers. As we have already seen, comparative lawyers may have quite similar interests to sociologists of law or legal historians and may draw on empirical work about how law is used in various societies or on historical work about how legal systems have changed over time. Because comparativists are ultimately interested in the law in action, interdisciplinary work is often important for comparative legal research. In many ways, as we noted at the beginning of this chapter, comparative approaches to the study of law cut across and overlap with the other approaches outlined in this book.

What makes comparative legal research reasonably distinct, however, is the stress placed on the comparison of legal systems or rules. To a large degree, comparative legal research is a matter of this comparative method. Two broad methods can be distinguished—macro-comparison and micro-comparison. Macro-comparison is the comparison of two or more legal systems in the narrower sense of that term (i.e. countries) or the broader sense (i.e. traditions). Micro-comparison refers to the comparison of a particular aspect of two or more legal systems. For example, to compare the sources of law of one legal system with another is a form of micro-comparison. In terms of micro-comparison, it has been argued that the search for "functional equivalence" (that is, finding things that do the same job) is the basic methodological pattern of comparative law because ultimately every legal system faces the same social, economic and political problems. These problems may be solved by different means or laws. For example, a comparative lawyer might ask what is the functional equivalent of the English contract in Scots law or French law. This may lead him or her to notice that "consideration"[1] is required in English contract law but not in Scots or French law. A deeper and broader analysis of the issue might raise interesting sociological questions—why does English law insist on consideration where Scots or French law does not? Does this mean that

English people have less of a sense that their word is their bond than Scots? Does it mean that one law grew from something different?

POTENTIAL PITFALLS

There are many potential pitfalls for the new comparativist (and indeed for the older one). Many of them come down to the problems created by imposing the scholar's own preconceptions onto a different legal system. For example, there are critiques of the search for functional equivalence. One critique suggests that comparative lawyers are misguided in this search because it leads to a bias towards finding things which are similar—the argument is that comparative lawyers should be more open to recognising difference in other legal systems. To take a simple example, the fact of death creates the need to transmit property from one generation to another. In common law systems, this is managed by means of the will and the doctrine of testamentary freedom (now somewhat reduced by the possibility of family provision in some jurisdictions) which allows a person to make a will which passes the property on death. In civilian systems, there is a systematic pattern of forced inheritance, in that the state prescribes who should take what property, and the scope for a will may be limited to a third or less of the estate. In both these systems this transmission occurs on death. But in some African societies, property passes to the next generation at the time a person becomes old enough to join in communal holding—so that death is not the precipitating event even though inter-generational transfer is happening. It is easy to see that the civil and common law systems are dealing with the same issue; not quite so easy to see the African system as dealing with it as well.

Equally, a bias towards finding similarity may lead researchers to miss or overlook things that are important. Thus, to conclude, as some did in the past, that chthonic legal systems such as those of Australian Aboriginal people were not law was to assume that law could only operate where there were formal courts, recognisable lawyers and buildings to house them in and so on. However, if it becomes clear that Aboriginal people are required to do things according to law and may be punished by a community action if they do not, then it can be seen that this is a legal system.

A related difficulty is that the labelling or classifying of law by one legal system may mislead the comparative lawyer into thinking that a functional equivalent does not exist in another he or she is examining. If one wishes to compare "land law" in two systems there may be a problem if the systems classify differently. For example, not all legal systems would regard a lease as personalty (that is personal property or goods as opposed to land) as the common law does. So to compare what is labelled "land law" could be problematic. It is important to be clear about exactly which aspect of law is being considered and try to confine statements within the limits of this and a specific context. There are real dangers in making over-large statements. In the example above one might have to decide whether what is being studied in the systems being compared is the law concerning the thing we call land, and we would have to decide whether that includes only earth or also fixtures on the land etc; or whether we were going to study what each system meant by their term "land law". The outcome might be different depending on which topic is chosen.

Further difficulties are created by the problem of language. What translations of law should be relied on if one does not speak or read the language of the legal system being compared? Unless an official translation is available there will be problems with interpretations of particular words or phrases. Indeed, one of the major problems of translation is that languages usually cannot be translated with 1:1 precision. A further difficulty may be created by the fact that secondary materials might also have relied on unofficial translations. When one considers that in many places law is a language-based discipline whose operation relies on very fine distinctions, it is clear that comparative legal research can be very difficult.

Finally, it is very important to remember that legal systems are dynamic. The comparative scholar will usually need to look at the history of the law in question in order to have some sense of how it works within its context.

## USES OF COMPARATIVE LEGAL RESEARCH

At one level we might argue that comparative legal research has an intrinsic interest which feeds our curiosity as students and scholars about the legal world beyond our own little corners. However, beyond this it is generally recognised that comparative work serves three basic purposes.

### Enriching understanding of one's own system
We have already mentioned that comparative law can enrich one's understanding of one's own legal system. Knowledge of other legal systems can prevent one from making assumptions that there is only one way to approach an issue. Beyond this, it can show us ways in which our own system is defective; it can show us ways proposed legal solutions have operated elsewhere and alert us to likely pitfalls and advantages. As globalisation and political communities such as the European Union have developed, the understanding of other legal systems has become ever more important and comparative law scholarship has grown as a result.

### For the purpose of transplant or law reform
It is common for legal systems to consider other countries' laws for the purposes of law reform. For example, the jury is regarded as a creature of the common law system. Recently the jury has been studied by a number of Asian civil law systems with a view to incorporating it into their criminal justice system. For example, the jury was introduced in Japan in 2009 after a comprehensive comparative law study of uses of the jury. Obvious issues arise when rules or laws from one system are transplanted to another. There may be unintended consequences because the context of the law will be different in the new system. However, a systematic study of how different

legal solutions have operated within similar stages of economic or social development or when particular crisis points arose allows the transplant of laws or law reform with fewer unintended consequences.

**For the purposes of harmonisation or unification**
We have already discussed the study of comparative law for the purposes of harmonisation in Europe. In Europe there are a number of harmonisation projects, including in European tort law. Objectives of this project have varied from harmonisation to the point where a European Civil Code might be developed, to the idea that differences should be maintained where they exist although where there is commonality that should be emphasised. The European Product Liability Directive is an example of common principles which have been turned into a directive which all must follow. In the United States the Restatements which are issued by the American Law Institute require comparative study of the law of each of the States before a Restatement of the law is issued which sets out a harmonised or unified statement of the law. Particularly where there are federations, such as in the United States, Australia or Canada, or where there is a devolution of powers as in the United Kingdom, comparative law can be done within the one polity.

CONCLUSION

Comparative law offers a rich approach to the understanding of both one's own legal system and that of others. All the areas of comparative law discussed above have value for the greater understanding of law generally. However, equally, as the world gets "smaller" it also becomes important for a wide range of human activities to have greater understanding of other peoples' law. As time passes and the world seems to become ever-more connected, the need for such understanding simply increases. This chapter has attempted to introduce most of the issues and concepts required for a basic understanding of comparative law. It has also sought to show that the first statement made in the chapter, that comparative law seems like a fascinating subject, is absolutely true.

FURTHER READING

De Cruz, Peter, *Comparative Law in a Changing World*, 3rd edn (Abingdon: Routledge–Cavendish, 2007).
Glenn, H. Patrick, *Legal Traditions of the World*, 4th edn (1st edn 2000) (Oxford: Oxford University Press, 2010).
Glendon, M., Carozza P., Picker, C., *Comparative Legal Traditions: Text, Materials and Cases on Western Law*, 3rd edn (Thomson/West, 2007).
Zweigert, K. and Kotz, H., *Einführung in die Rechtsvergleichung*, 3e Aufl (Tübingen: Mohr, 1996). English translation: *Introduction to comparative law*, translated from the German by Tony Weir (Oxford: Clarendon Press, 1998).

Watson, A., *Legal transplants: an approach to comparative law* (Edinburgh: Scottish Academic Press, 1974), reprinted with new afterword 1993 by University of Georgia Press. The titles of the first three chapters are interesting: *Comparative law as an academic discipline, The perils of comparative law,* and *The virtues of comparative law.*

---

[1] At common law, in order for a contract to be considered valid it must include "consideration". Consideration is some money or other benefit accruing to one party or some loss or responsibility suffered by the other party.

# INDEX